# TRADITIONAL
# ITALIAN

**THE AUSTRALIAN Women's Weekly**

D1581231

# contents

antipasto                           4

soups                               16

pasta                               22

rice and polenta                    38

meat and poultry                    48

seafood                             68

salads and vegetables              84

pizza and breads                    92

desserts                           104

glossary                           116

index                              118

conversion chart                   119

From bruschetta to tiramisu, traditional Italian food is one of the world's most well-known and most eaten cuisines, and it's also one that so many of you have adopted as practically native to your own repertoire. This book helps make getting an Italian feast on the table easy: with many of the most universally loved recipes, stated simply and illustrated beautifully, in one concise compendium, it will inspire you to get a terrific Italian feast on the table in very little time, and even less effort. Mangiamo!

Pamela Clark

# fig and fetta mini toasts

**preparation time** 10 minutes (plus refrigeration time) **makes** 24

1 tablespoon finely chopped fresh chives

24 melba toasts

3 medium fresh figs (180g)

MARINATED FETTA

1 teaspoon finely grated lemon rind

2 teaspoons fresh thyme leaves

1 clove garlic, crushed

125g fetta, cut into 12 pieces

¾ cup (180ml) olive oil

1   Make marinated fetta.
2   Using fork, mash cheese with chives in small bowl; spread on one side of each toast.
3   Cut each fig into eight wedges; place one wedge on each toast. Sprinkle with coarsely ground black pepper, if desired.

MARINATED FETTA  Combine rind, thyme and garlic in small sterilised glass jar with tight-fitting lid; add cheese. Seal jar, shake gently to coat cheese in mixture. Open jar and pour in enough of the oil to completely cover cheese mixture. Reseal; refrigerate overnight.

TIPS  Make double quantity of marinated fetta and store remainder in refrigerator for up to two weeks. Marinated fetta is great tossed in salads or as a spread on sandwiches.

PER SERVING  8.3g fat; 410kJ (98 cal)

ANTIPASTO

# bruschetta with eggplant and olive topping

**preparation time** 15 minutes  **cooking time** 10 minutes  **serves** 4

*Buy char-grilled eggplant and capsicum at your favourite delicatessen.*

1 tablespoon extra virgin olive oil

1 small white onion (80g), chopped finely

2 cloves garlic, crushed

1 trimmed celery stalk (100g), chopped finely

150g char-grilled eggplant, chopped finely

150g char-grilled red capsicum, chopped finely

¼ cup (40g) pitted black olives, chopped coarsely

1 tablespoon drained baby capers

2 tablespoons toasted pine nuts

¼ cup finely shredded fresh basil

350g loaf ciabatta

2 tablespoons extra virgin olive oil, extra

1  Heat oil in medium frying pan; cook onion, garlic and celery, stirring, until onion softens. Transfer onion mixture to medium bowl.

2  Add eggplant, capsicum, olives, capers, pine nuts and basil to onion mixture; mix well.

3  Cut bread on slight angle into eight slices. Brush one side of bread slices with extra oil; grill on both sides until toasted.

4  Top toast with eggplant mixture; sprinkle with extra basil leaves, if desired.

**PER SERVING**  33.5g fat; 2362kJ (565 cal)

# carpaccio with fennel salad

**preparation time** 10 minutes (plus freezing time) **serves** 4

400g beef eye fillet

2 medium fennel bulbs (600g)

2 trimmed celery stalks (150g)

2 tablespoons finely chopped fresh flat-leaf parsley

2 tablespoons lemon juice

1 clove garlic, crushed

¼ teaspoon white sugar

½ teaspoon dijon mustard

⅓ cup (80ml) olive oil

1 Remove any excess fat from fillet, wrap tightly in plastic wrap; freeze about 1 hour or until partially frozen. Using sharp knife, slice fillet as thinly as possible.

2 Meanwhile, slice fennel and celery thinly; toss in medium bowl with remaining ingredients.

3 Arrange carpaccio slices in single layer on serving plates; top with fennel salad. Serve accompanied with sliced Italian bread, if desired.

**PER SERVING** 24.4g fat; 1379kJ (330 cal)

# warm olives with garlic, chilli and oregano

**preparation time** 5 minutes  **cooking time** 5 minutes  **serves** 8

¾ cup (180ml) extra virgin olive oil

1 fresh long red chilli, sliced thinly

1 clove garlic, sliced thinly

¼ cup coarsely chopped fresh oregano leaves

250g black olives

250g green olives

1 Gently heat olive oil in a large frying pan with the chilli, garlic and oregano until warm and fragrant.

2 Add olives; shake pan until olives are heated through.

3 Serve olives with grissini (thin Italian bread sticks), if desired.

**PER SERVING** 21.0g fat; 974kJ (233 cal)

# frittata with two toppings

2 tablespoons extra virgin olive oil

1 medium brown onion (150g), chopped finely

2 tablespoons coarsely chopped
fresh flat-leaf parsley

2 tablespoons finely grated parmesan

10 eggs, beaten lightly

20g butter

2 cloves garlic, crushed

8 button mushrooms (100g)

4 char-grilled artichokes, halved

¼ cup (50g) char-grilled capsicum, sliced thinly

1   Heat oil in medium frying pan; cook onion, stirring, until soft.
    Stir in half of the parsley.

2   Combine cheese and eggs in medium bowl; pour into pan. Cook
    over low heat, covered loosely with foil, about 8 minutes or until
    edges are set.

3   Place pan under a preheated grill until browned lightly and just set.
    Invert onto a board.

4   Meanwhile, heat butter in small frying pan; cook garlic and
    mushrooms, stirring, until just tender; stir in remaining parsley.

5   Cut frittata into 16 wedges, arrange on serving platter. Top half
    the wedges with mushroom mixture and half with artichokes
    and capsicum.

**PER SERVING**  14.4g fat; 736kJ (176 cal)

ANTIPASTO

11

# marinated eggplants

**preparation time** 15 minutes  (plus standing time)  **cooking time** 5 minutes  **makes** 1 litre (4 cups)

10 medium baby eggplants (600g)

coarse cooking salt

1 litre (4 cups) white vinegar

2 cups (500ml) water

2 teaspoons salt, extra

½ teaspoon dried thyme

1 clove garlic, sliced thinly

1 fresh small red chilli, seeded, chopped

½ teaspoon cracked black pepper

1½ cups (375ml) hot olive oil, approximately

1   Cut eggplants into quarters lengthways; place eggplant in colander, sprinkle with salt, stand 1 hour. Rinse eggplant under cold water; drain on absorbent paper.

2   Heat vinegar, the water and extra salt in medium saucepan until hot (do not boil). Add eggplant; simmer gently, uncovered, 5 minutes. Drain; discard vinegar mixture.

3   Combine thyme, garlic, chilli, pepper and hot oil in heatproof bowl. Place eggplant upright in sterilised 1-litre (4-cup) jar; carefully top with enough oil mixture to cover eggplant, leaving 1cm space between eggplant and top of jar. Seal while hot.

**TIP**   Store in refrigerator for up to three months.

**PER SERVING**  12.7g fat; 512kJ (122 cal)

# marinated mushrooms

**preparation time** 10 minutes  **cooking time** 5 minutes  **makes** 1 litre (4 cups)

1 litre (4 cups) white vinegar

2 cups (500ml) water

2 teaspoons salt

800g button mushrooms

2 teaspoons dried parsley

½ teaspoon dried thyme

1 clove garlic, sliced thinly

½ teaspoon cracked black pepper

1½ cups (375ml) hot olive oil, approximately

1   Heat vinegar, the water and salt in medium saucepan until hot (do not boil). Add mushrooms; simmer gently, uncovered, for 5 minutes. Drain; discard vinegar mixture.

2   Combine hot mushrooms, herbs, garlic and pepper in large heatproof bowl; mix well. Place mushroom mixture in sterilised 1-litre (4-cup) jar; carefully top with enough oil to completely cover mushrooms, leaving 1cm space between mushrooms and top of jar. Seal while hot.

**TIP**   Store in refrigerator for up to three months.

**PER SERVING**  10.8g fat; 452kJ (108 cal)

# marinated capsicums

**preparation time** 20 minutes  **cooking time** 20 minutes  **makes** 1 litre (4 cups)

3 medium red capsicums (600g)

3 medium yellow capsicums (600g)

1 litre (4 cups) white vinegar

2 cups (500ml) water

2 teaspoons salt

1 clove garlic, sliced thinly

½ teaspoon dried thyme

3 dried bay leaves

½ teaspoon cracked black pepper

1½ cups (375ml) hot olive oil, approximately

1   Remove seeds and membranes from capsicums; cut capsicums into 4cm strips. Heat vinegar, the water and salt in medium saucepan until hot (do not boil). Add capsicum; simmer gently, uncovered, for 15 minutes. Drain; discard vinegar mixture.

2   Combine hot capsicum, garlic, thyme, bay leaves and pepper in large heatproof bowl. Place capsicum mixture in sterilised 1-litre (4-cup) jar; carefully top with enough oil to cover capsicum, leaving 1cm space between capsicum and top of jar. Seal while hot.

**TIP**   Store in refrigerator for up to three months.

**PER SERVING**  10.1g fat; 429kJ (102 cal)

# herbed baked ricotta

**preparation time** 15 minutes  **cooking time** 1 hour (plus cooling time)  **serves** 8

1kg ricotta

2 tablespoons finely chopped fresh thyme

2 cloves garlic, crushed

2 eggs, beaten lightly

1 tablespoon finely chopped garlic chives

1 tablespoon finely grated lemon rind

1  Preheat oven to moderate (180°C/160°C fan-forced). Grease deep 20cm-round cake pan; line base with baking paper.

2  Place cheese in large bowl with thyme, garlic, egg, chives and rind; mix well. Spoon cheese mixture into prepared pan.

3  Bake, uncovered, about 1 hour or until browned lightly and firm to touch; cool in pan.

**TIP**  Baked ricotta can be refrigerated, covered, for up to three days.

**PER SERVING** 15.5g fat; 853kJ (204 cal)

# mussels with garlic crumbs

**preparation time** 20 minutes  **cooking time** 10 minutes  **serves** 8

1 cup (70g) stale breadcrumbs

2 cloves garlic, chopped finely

1 teaspoon finely grated lemon rind

2 tablespoons finely chopped
fresh flat-leaf parsley

1kg small black mussels

1½ cups (375ml) water

¼ cup (60ml) extra virgin olive oil

1  Combine breadcrumbs, garlic, rind and parsley in small bowl. Scrub mussels; remove beards.

2  Bring the water to a boil in large saucepan; add mussels. Boil, covered, about 7 minutes or until mussels open. (Discard any that do not.)

3  Fully open shells, discard tops. Loosen mussels from shells with a spoon; replace in shells. Place shells, in single layer, on large baking tray. Sprinkle with breadcrumb mixture; drizzle with oil. Cook under preheated grill about 3 minutes or until browned.

**PER SERVING** 7.6g fat; 477kJ (114 cal)

# minestrone alla milanese

**preparation time** 40 minutes (plus standing and refrigeration times) **cooking time** 3 hours 35 minutes **serves** 6

*There are as many versions of minestrone as there are regions in Italy; this recipe is based on a seasonal soup made in Milan, the capital of the northern region of Lombardy, where the colder winters seem to inspire hearty fare such as this. Rice, rather than pasta or bread, is used as a thickener, and the ham hocks impart a pleasing smoky flavour that seems to fight the chill.*

⅓ cup (130g) dried borlotti beans

2 ham hocks (1kg)

1 medium brown onion (150g), chopped coarsely

1 trimmed celery stalk (100g), chopped coarsely

1 teaspoon black peppercorns

1 bay leaf

3 medium carrots (360g), chopped coarsely

4 litres (16 cups) water

1 tablespoon olive oil

1 large white onion (200g), chopped coarsely

3 cloves garlic, crushed

4 small tomatoes (360g), peeled, chopped coarsely

1 tablespoon tomato paste

2 trimmed celery stalks (200g), chopped coarsely, extra

2 medium potatoes (400g), chopped coarsely

½ small cabbage (600g), shredded coarsely

2 medium zucchini (240g), chopped coarsely

½ cup (100g) arborio rice

¼ cup finely chopped fresh flat-leaf parsley

2 tablespoons finely shredded fresh basil leaves

1 Place beans in medium bowl, cover with water; stand overnight, drain. Rinse under cold water; drain.

2 Preheat oven to hot (200°C/180°C fan-forced).

3 Roast ham hocks and onion on oven tray, uncovered, 30 minutes. Combine ham hocks and brown onion with celery, peppercorns, bay leaf, a third of the carrot and the water in large saucepan. Bring to a boil then reduce heat; simmer, uncovered, 2 hours. Strain stock through muslin-lined sieve or colander into large bowl; discard solids. Allow stock to cool; cover, refrigerate until cold.

4 Heat oil in large saucepan; cook white onion and garlic, stirring, until onion softens. Discard fat from surface of stock. Add stock, beans and tomato to pan with tomato paste, extra celery, potato and remaining carrot. Bring to a boil then reduce heat; simmer, covered, about 40 minutes or until beans are just tender.

5 Add cabbage, zucchini and rice; simmer, uncovered, about 15 minutes or until rice is just tender. Stir in parsley and basil just before serving.

**PER SERVING** 3.6g fat; 790kJ (189 cal)

SOUPS

# tuscan bean soup

**preparation time** 15 minutes  **cooking time** 2 hours 30 minutes  **serves** 6

2 tablespoons olive oil

3 medium brown onions (450g), chopped coarsely

2 cloves garlic, crushed

200g speck, chopped coarsely

2 medium carrots (240g), chopped coarsely

2 trimmed celery stalks (200g), chopped coarsely

2 x 400g cans tomatoes

¼ medium savoy cabbage (375g), shredded coarsely

1 medium zucchini (120g), chopped coarsely

2 sprigs fresh thyme

2 cups (500ml) beef stock

2 litres (8 cups) water

400g can borlotti beans, rinsed, drained

6 thick slices ciabatta

1  Heat oil in large saucepan. Add onion, garlic and speck; cook, stirring, about 5 minutes or until onion softens.

2  Add carrot, celery, undrained crushed tomatoes, cabbage, zucchini, thyme, stock and the water. Bring to a boil then reduce heat; simmer, uncovered, 2 hours.

3  Add beans; simmer, uncovered, 20 minutes.

4  Meanwhile, toast or grill bread. Stand a slice of bread in the base of six serving bowls, top with soup. Drizzle with extra olive oil, if desired.

**TIP**  Substitute bacon or pancetta for speck.

**PER SERVING**  8.9g fat; 1272kJ (304 cal)


# stracciatella

**preparation time** 5 minutes  **cooking time** 10 minutes  **serves** 6

*Stracciatella, when translated from Italian to English, means strings or torn rags. This satisfying soup is thus aptly named, since this is what the parmesan-and-egg mixture resembles once it meets the hot stock.*

5 eggs

½ cup (40g) finely grated parmesan

1.5 litres (6 cups) chicken stock

2 tablespoons finely chopped fresh flat-leaf parsley

Pinch nutmeg

1  Lightly whisk eggs with cheese in medium jug until combined.

2  Bring stock to a boil in large saucepan. Remove from heat; gradually add egg mixture, whisking constantly.

3  Return mixture to heat; simmer, stirring constantly, about 5 minutes or until egg mixture forms fine shreds. Stir in parsley and nutmeg.

**PER SERVING**  6.9g fat; 606kJ (145 cal)

# seafood soup with gremolata

**preparation time** 30 minutes  **cooking time** 1 hour 20 minutes  **serves** 6

2kg fish bones

1 medium brown onion (150g), chopped coarsely

1 medium carrot (120g), chopped coarsely

2 trimmed celery stalks (150g), chopped coarsely

4 litres (16 cups) water

8 black peppercorns

2 bay leaves

1 tablespoon olive oil

1 medium brown onion (150g), chopped coarsely, extra

2 cloves garlic, crushed

5 medium tomatoes (950g), chopped

3 teaspoons white sugar

400g can tomatoes

¼ cup (60g) tomato paste

½ cup (125ml) dry white wine

2 medium uncooked lobster tails (760g), shelled, chopped coarsely

400g boneless firm white fish fillets, chopped coarsely

GREMOLATA

1 clove garlic, chopped finely

1 tablespoon finely chopped lemon rind

2 tablespoons finely chopped fresh flat-leaf parsley

1  Combine fish bones, onion, carrot, celery, the water, peppercorns and bay leaves in large saucepan. Bring to a boil then reduce heat; simmer, uncovered, 20 minutes. Strain stock over large bowl; discard bones and vegetables.

2  Heat oil in large saucepan; cook extra onion and garlic, stirring, until onion softens. Add chopped tomato and sugar; cook, stirring, about 10 minutes or until tomato is soft. Stir in undrained crushed tomatoes, paste and wine. Bring to a boil then reduce heat; simmer, uncovered, about 5 minutes or until mixture has thickened slightly, stirring occasionally. Add stock, bring to a boil. Reduce heat; simmer, uncovered, 20 minutes. Cool 10 minutes.

3  Make gremolata. Blend or process tomato mixture, in batches, until pureed; return to same cleaned pan, bring to a boil. Add lobster and fish; simmer, stirring, about 5 minutes or until seafood is just cooked.

4  Divide soup between serving bowls; sprinkle each serving with gremolata.

**GREMOLATA**  Combine ingredients in small bowl.

**PER SERVING**  6.6g fat; 1232kJ (295 cal)

## spaghetti napoletana

**preparation time** 10 minutes  **cooking time** 45 minutes  **serves** 2

2 x 400g cans tomatoes

30g butter

1 tablespoon olive oil

2 cloves garlic, crushed

1 tablespoon shredded fresh basil

2 tablespoons chopped fresh flat-leaf parsley

250g spaghetti

1  Push tomatoes, with their liquid, through sieve.

2  Heat butter and oil in large saucepan, add garlic; cook, stirring, 1 minute. Add pureed tomato; bring to a boil. Reduce heat; simmer, uncovered, about 40 minutes or until sauce reduces by about half. Stir in basil and parsley.

3  Meanwhile, cook pasta in large saucepan of boiling water, uncovered, until just tender; drain. Combine sauce and pasta.

**PER SERVING**  23.6g fat; 2750kJ (658 cal)

# fettuccine carbonara

**preparation time** 10 minutes **cooking time** 10 minutes **serves** 4

*Named for a pasta sauce made by Italian charcoal-makers, and so easy to prepare it could be whipped up in a single pot hung over a fire out in the forest, carbonara has come to represent the classic, easy, creamy pasta sauce. You can use pancetta or prosciutto instead of the bacon if you prefer.*

4 bacon rashers (280g), chopped coarsely

375g fettuccine

3 egg yolks, beaten lightly

1 cup (250ml) cream

½ cup (30g) finely grated parmesan

2 tablespoons coarsely chopped fresh chives

1　Cook bacon in heated small frying pan, stirring, until crisp; drain.

2　Meanwhile, cook pasta in large saucepan of boiling water, uncovered, until just tender; drain.

3　Combine hot pasta in large bowl with egg yolks, cream, cheese and bacon; sprinkle with chives.

TIP　Try using grated romano or pepato instead of parmesan.

**PER SERVING**　34.2g fat; 2762kJ (661 cal)

# penne puttanesca with mushrooms

**preparation time** 15 minutes **cooking time** 15 minutes **serves** 4

1 tablespoon olive oil

1 large brown onion (200g), sliced thinly

2 cloves garlic, crushed

6 anchovy fillets, drained, chopped coarsely

250g mushrooms, quartered

1 fresh small red chilli, sliced thinly

⅔ cup (160ml) dry white wine

600g bottled tomato pasta sauce

500g penne

⅔ cup (110g) seeded kalamata olives, quartered lengthways

1 tablespoon drained capers, rinsed

¼ cup coarsely chopped fresh flat-leaf parsley

1　Heat oil in large saucepan; cook onion and garlic, stirring, until onion softens. Add anchovy, mushrooms and chilli; cook, stirring, 2 minutes. Stir in wine and sauce. Bring to a boil then reduce heat; simmer, uncovered, about 5 minutes or until sauce thickens slightly.

2　Meanwhile, cook pasta in large saucepan of boiling water, uncovered, until just tender; drain.

3　Add pasta to sauce with remaining ingredients; toss to combine.

**PER SERVING**　8.1g fat; 2656kJ (645 cal)

# lasagne bolognese

**preparation time** 1 hour 15 minutes **cooking time** 2 hours 45 minutes (plus standing time) **serves** 8

*This is the way lasagne is traditionally made in Bologna – with chicken liver and milk in the sauce. Semolina flour is made from crushed durum wheat hearts, ground to a very fine flour. It is available at most supermarkets and health food stores.*

2 teaspoons olive oil

6 slices pancetta (90g), chopped finely

1 large white onion (200g), chopped finely

1 medium carrot (120g), chopped finely

2 trimmed celery stalks (200g), chopped finely

1kg beef mince

150g chicken livers, trimmed, chopped finely

2 cups (500ml) milk

60g butter

2 cups (500ml) beef stock

1 cup (250ml) dry red wine

410g can tomato puree

2 tablespoons tomato paste

¼ cup finely chopped fresh flat-leaf parsley

2 cups (160g) finely grated parmesan

PASTA

1 cup (150g) plain flour

¼ cup (45g) semolina flour

2 eggs

1 tablespoon olive oil

semolina flour, for dusting, extra

WHITE SAUCE

125g butter

¾ cup (110g) plain flour

1.25 litres (5 cups) hot milk

1 Heat oil in large heavy-based pan; cook pancetta, stirring, until crisp. Add onion, carrot and celery; cook, stirring, until vegetables soften. Add beef and liver; cook, stirring, until beef just changes colour. Stir in milk and butter; cook, stirring occasionally, until liquid reduces to about half. Add stock, wine, puree and paste; simmer, uncovered, 1½ hours. Remove from heat; stir in parsley.

2 Meanwhile, make pasta.

3 Preheat oven to moderately hot (200°C/180°C fan-forced). Grease deep 26cm x 35cm baking dish.

4 Make white sauce. Spread about ½ cup of the white sauce over base of dish. Layer two pasta sheets, a quarter of the meat sauce, ¼ cup of the cheese and about 1 cup of the remaining white sauce in dish. Repeat layering process, starting with pasta sheets and ending with white sauce; you will have four layers in total. Top lasagne with the remaining cheese.

5 Bake lasagne, uncovered, about 40 minutes or until top is browned lightly. Stand 15 minutes before cutting.

PASTA Process flours, eggs and oil until mixture forms a ball. Transfer dough to floured surface; knead about 5 minutes or until smooth. Divide dough into quarters; roll each piece through pasta machine set on thickest setting. Fold long sides of dough into the centre, roll through machine. Repeat rolling several times, adjusting setting so pasta sheets become thinner with each roll; dust pasta with extra semolina flour when necessary. Roll to second thinnest setting (1mm thick), making sure pasta is at least 10cm wide. Cut pasta into 35cm lengths. Cook pasta sheets in large saucepan of boiling salted water, in batches, about 1 minute or until pasta rises to surface. Transfer to bowl of iced water; drain, pat dry with absorbent paper towel.

WHITE SAUCE Melt butter in medium saucepan; add flour, stirring until mixture forms a smooth paste. Stir in milk gradually; bring to a boil, stirring, until sauce boils and thickens.

TIPS Fresh or dried lasagne sheets can be substituted for the homemade pasta. Bolognese can also be served with spaghetti.

PER SERVING 53.1g fat; 3657kJ (874 cal)

# grilled vegetables and basil tapenade pasta

**preparation time** 20 minutes **cooking time** 25 minutes **serves** 4

1 large eggplant (500g), sliced thickly

2 large zucchini (300g), sliced thickly

250g cherry tomatoes

375g tagliatelle

1 cup loosely packed fresh basil leaves

BASIL TAPENADE

2½ cups (300g) seeded black olives

2 tablespoons drained capers, rinsed

1 clove garlic, quartered

2 tablespoons lemon juice

¼ cup loosely packed fresh basil leaves

⅓ cup (80ml) olive oil

1　Make basil tapenade.

2　Cook eggplant, zucchini and tomatoes, in batches, on heated oiled grill plate (or grill or barbecue) until browned.

3　Meanwhile, cook pasta in large saucepan of boiling water, uncovered, until just tender; drain.

4　Place hot pasta in medium bowl with vegetables, tapenade and basil leaves; toss gently to combine.

BASIL TAPENADE　Blend or process ingredients until smooth.

TIPS　Making the tapenade using a mortar and pestle will give it a thick yet smooth texture. Try stirring a spoonful of tapenade into a pasta sauce or vegetable soup, spreading it on a slice of bruschetta or canapé base, or thinning it with mayonnaise for a dip or lemon and olive oil to flavour a mixed salad.

**PER SERVING** 20.7g fat; 25.4kJ (599 cal)

# orecchiette boscaiola

**preparation time** 10 minutes **cooking time** 10 minutes **serves** 4

375g orecchiette

60g butter

135g pancetta, chopped finely

150g mushrooms, sliced thinly

1 clove garlic, crushed

1 teaspoon cracked black pepper

300ml cream

½ cup (40g) finely grated parmesan

1　Cook pasta in large saucepan of boiling water, uncovered, until just tender; drain.

2　Melt butter in medium frying pan; cook pancetta, stirring, 5 minutes. Add mushrooms and garlic; cook, stirring, 3 minutes.

3　Add pepper and cream; simmer, uncovered, about 5 minutes or until sauce reduces by half.

4　Add cheese; stir over low heat, about 2 minutes or until cheese melts. Combine pasta and sauce in a large bowl.

**PER SERVING** 52.7g fat; 2232kJ (534 cal)

# chilli and garlic spaghettini with breadcrumbs

**preparation time** 10 minutes  **cooking time** 10 minutes  **serves** 4

375g spaghettini

⅓ cup (80ml) olive oil

50g butter

4 cloves garlic, crushed

4 fresh small red chillies, seeded, chopped finely

2 cups (140g) stale breadcrumbs

½ cup coarsely chopped fresh flat-leaf parsley

2 teaspoons finely grated lemon rind

1 Cook pasta in large saucepan of boiling water, uncovered, until just tender; drain.

2 Meanwhile, heat half the oil in large frying pan with butter until butter melts. Add garlic, chilli and breadcrumbs; cook, stirring, until breadcrumbs are browned lightly.

3 Combine drained hot pasta and breadcrumb mixture in large bowl with parsley, lemon rind and remaining oil.

**PER SERVING** 30.9g fat; 2916kJ (697 cal)

# spaghetti with clams

**preparation time** 15 minutes (plus 1 hour standing time)  **cooking time** 15 minutes  **serves** 4

1kg clams

¼ cup (60ml) dry white wine

500g spaghetti

½ cup (125ml) extra virgin olive oil

2 cloves garlic, crushed

2 fresh medium red chillies, chopped

½ cup coarsely chopped fresh flat-leaf parsley

1 Rinse clams. Place in a bowl of cold water for 1 hour to purge any grit; drain.

2 Place wine in large saucepan; bring to a boil. Add clams; simmer, covered, until shells open. (Discard any that do not.) Remove clams from pan; cover to keep warm. Strain cooking liquid through fine sieve into a jug; reserve ½ cup (125ml) of the liquid.

3 Cook pasta in a large saucepan of boiling water, uncovered, until just tender; drain. Return pasta to pan.

4 Meanwhile, heat oil in small frying pan; add garlic and chilli; cook, stirring, until fragrant. Add clams to pasta with oil mixture, parsley and enough of reserved cooking liquid to moisten; toss gently.

**PER SERVING** 30.1g fat; 3043kJ (728 cal)

# chicken and prosciutto cannelloni

**preparation time** 30 minutes  **cooking time** 1 hour 10 minutes  **serves** 8

50g butter

¼ cup (35g) plain flour

⅔ cup (160ml) milk

1½ cups (375ml) chicken stock

½ cup (40g) finely grated parmesan

400g fontina, grated coarsely

1 tablespoon olive oil

2 medium brown onions (300g), chopped finely

3 cloves garlic, crushed

1 kg chicken mince

2 tablespoons finely chopped fresh sage

850g canned tomatoes

½ cup (125ml) dry white wine

¼ cup (70g) tomato paste

3 teaspoons white sugar

12 fresh lasagne sheets

24 slices prosciutto (360g)

1   Heat butter in medium saucepan; cook flour, stirring, until mixture bubbles and thickens. Gradually stir in milk and stock; cook, stirring, until sauce boils and thickens. Remove from heat; stir in parmesan and a quarter of the fontina.

2   Heat oil in large saucepan; cook onion and garlic, stirring, until onion softens. Add chicken; cook, stirring, until browned. Stir in sage. Combine chicken and cheese sauce in large bowl; cool.

3   Combine undrained crushed tomatoes, wine, paste and sugar in same large pan; cook, stirring, 10 minutes. Cool 10 minutes; blend or process, in batches, until smooth.

4   Preheat oven to moderate (180°C/160°C fan-forced).

5   Cut pasta sheets and prosciutto slices in half crossways. Place two pieces of prosciutto on each piece of pasta. Top each piece of pasta with ¼ cup chicken mixture; roll to enclose filling.

6   Oil two 3-litre (12-cup) ovenproof dishes. Pour a quarter of the tomato sauce into base of each prepared dish; place half of the pasta rolls, seam-side down, in each dish. Pour remaining tomato sauce over rolls; sprinkle each dish with remaining fontina.

7   Bake cannelloni, covered, 30 minutes. Uncover, bake further 15 minutes or until cheese melts and browns. Serve with a green salad, if desired.

**TIP** Pancetta or double-smoked ham can be substituted for the prosciutto.

**PER SERVING** 40.3g fat; 2998kJ (717 cal)

PASTA

**33**

# gnocchi with three sauces

**preparation time** 30 minutes (plus refrigeration time) **cooking time** 25 minutes **serves** 8

*Each of the following sauce recipes makes enough to accompany the gnocchi recipe below.*

1kg potatoes, unpeeled

2 eggs, beaten lightly

30g butter, melted

¼ cup (20g) finely grated parmesan

2 cups (300g) plain flour, approximately

1   Boil or steam whole potatoes until tender; drain. Peel when cool enough to handle. Mash, using ricer, mouli or fine sieve and wooden spoon, into large bowl; stir in eggs, butter, parmesan and enough of the flour to make a firm dough.

2   Divide dough into eight equal parts; roll each part on lightly floured surface into 2cm-thick sausage shape. Cut each sausage shape into 2cm pieces; roll pieces into balls.

3   Roll each ball along the inside tines of a fork, pressing lightly on top of ball with index finger to form classic gnocchi shape – grooves on one side and a dimple on the other. Place gnocchi, in single layer, on lightly floured tray, cover; refrigerate 1 hour.

4   Cook gnocchi in large saucepan of boiling water, uncovered, about 3 minutes or until gnocchi float to the surface. Remove from pan with slotted spoon; drain. Serve hot, with the sauce of your choice.

TIPS   Potato should be mashed while hot but can be cooled slightly before being mixed with remaining ingredients. We used russet burbank potatoes in this recipe.

**PER SERVING** 5.8g fat; 1079kJ (258 cal)

## classic pesto

**preparation time** 10 minutes
**cooking time** 5 minutes

2 cloves garlic, quartered

¼ cup (40g) toasted pine nuts

¼ cup (20g) finely grated parmesan

1 cup firmly packed fresh basil leaves

⅓ cup (80ml) olive oil

½ cup (125ml) cream

1   Blend or process garlic, pine nuts, cheese and basil until finely chopped. With motor operating, gradually add oil until pesto thickens.

2   Just before serving, transfer pesto to small saucepan. Add cream; stirring, over low heat, until heated through.

**PER SERVING (WITHOUT GNOCCHI)** 20.5g fat; 807kJ (193 cal)

## three-cheese sauce

**preparation time** 10 minutes
**cooking time** 15 minutes

60g butter

⅓ cup (50g) plain flour

2 cups (500ml) milk

300ml cream

60g coarsely grated provolone

70g coarsely grated fontina

40g gorgonzola, crumbled

1    Melt butter in medium saucepan. Add flour;
      cook, stirring, until mixture bubbles and
      thickens. Gradually add milk and cream; stir
      until mixture boils and thickens. Remove from
      heat; stir in cheeses.

**TIP** This sauce must be made just before serving.

**PER SERVING (WITHOUT GNOCCHI)** 31.1g fat;
    1446kJ (345 cal)

## tomato sauce

**preparation time** 10 minutes
**cooking time** 35 minutes

2 tablespoons olive oil

1 large brown onion (200g), chopped finely

2 cloves garlic, crushed

2 tablespoons tomato paste

2 x 425g cans crushed tomatoes

¼ cup finely shredded fresh basil leaves

1    Heat oil in medium heavy-based saucepan; cook
      onion and garlic, stirring, until onion softens.

2    Add tomato paste; cook, stirring, 1 minute. Stir
      in undrained tomatoes; bring to a boil. Reduce
      heat; simmer, uncovered, about 30 minutes or
      until sauce thickens slightly. Stir in basil.

**PER SERVING (WITHOUT GNOCCHI)** 5g fat; 299kJ
    (71 cal)

# vegetable gnocchi with cheese sauce

**preparation time** 2 hours (plus refrigeration time)   **cooking time** 40 minutes   **serves** 6

1.2kg potatoes

1 medium kumara (400g)

300g spinach, trimmed, chopped coarsely

3 eggs

½ cup (40g) coarsely grated parmesan

2 cups (300g) plain flour

2 tablespoons olive oil

100g blue cheese, crumbled

⅓ cup (25g) finely grated pecorino

CHEESE SAUCE

30g butter

2 tablespoons plain flour

2½ cups (625ml) milk

⅔ cup (160ml) cream

½ cup (50g) finely grated gruyère

⅔ cup (50g) finely grated pecorino

1  Boil or steam unpeeled potatoes until tender; drain. Peel when cool enough to handle; chop coarsely.

2  Meanwhile, microwave unpeeled kumara on HIGH (100%) about 8 minutes or until tender; drain. Peel when cool enough to handle. Boil, steam or microwave spinach until wilted; drain.

3  Using wooden spoon, push potato through fine sieve or mouli into large bowl. Divide potato mash among three medium bowls; stir one egg into each bowl until mixture is combined. Using wooden spoon, push kumara through fine sieve into one of the bowls; stir to combine. Stir parmesan into second bowl and spinach into the third; stir to combine. Add approximately ⅓ cup of flour to each bowl; stir each potato mixture to make a firm dough.

4  Roll each portion of dough on lightly floured surface into 2cm-thick sausage shape. Cut each sausage shape into 2cm pieces; roll pieces into balls. Roll each ball along the inside tines of a fork, pressing lightly on top of ball with index finger to form classic gnocchi shape – grooves on one side and a dimple on the other. Place gnocchi, in single layer, on lightly floured trays, cover; refrigerate 1 hour.

5  Cook gnocchi, uncovered, in large saucepan of boiling water about 2 minutes or until gnocchi float to surface. Remove from pan with slotted spoon; drain. Toss gnocchi in large bowl with oil.

6  Make cheese sauce. Pour sauce over gnocchi; toss gently to coat. Divide gnocchi among six lightly oiled 1½-cup (375ml) ovenproof dishes; sprinkle with blue cheese then pecorino. Place under hot grill about 3 minutes or until cheese browns lightly.

**CHEESE SAUCE**  Melt butter in medium saucepan. Add flour; cook, stirring, until mixture thickens and bubbles. Gradually add milk and cream; stir until mixture boils and thickens. Remove from heat; stir in cheeses.

**TIPS**  It's a good idea to cook the kumara in the microwave oven to keep water absorption to the minimum. We used russet burbank potatoes for this recipe.

**PER SERVING** 40.9g fat; 3313kJ (791 cal)

# prawn and asparagus risotto

**preparation time** 25 minutes  **cooking time** 45 minutes  **serves** 4

---

500g uncooked medium king prawns

3 cups (750ml) chicken stock

3 cups (750ml) water

10g butter

1 tablespoon olive oil

1 small brown onion (80g), chopped finely

2 cups (400g) arborio rice

½ cup (125ml) dry sherry

10g butter, extra

2 teaspoons olive oil, extra

2 cloves garlic, crushed

500g asparagus, chopped coarsely

⅓ cup (25g) coarsely grated parmesan

⅓ cup coarsely chopped fresh basil

1   Shell and devein prawns; chop prawn meat coarsely.

2   Place stock and the water in large saucepan. Bring to a boil then reduce heat; simmer, covered.

3   Meanwhile, heat butter and oil in large saucepan; cook onion, stirring, until soft. Add rice; stir to coat in onion mixture. Stir in sherry; cook, stirring, until sherry is absorbed.

4   Stir in ½ cup of the simmering stock mixture; cook, stirring, over low heat until stock is absorbed. Continue adding stock mixture, in ½-cup batches, stirring, until stock is absorbed after each addition. Total cooking time should be about 35 minutes or until rice is tender.

5   Heat extra butter and extra oil in medium frying pan; cook prawn meat and garlic, stirring, until prawn meat just changes colour.

6   Boil, steam or microwave asparagus until just tender; drain. Add asparagus, prawn mixture and cheese to risotto; cook, stirring, until cheese melts. Stir in basil.

**PER SERVING** 14.7g fat; 2516kJ (602 cal)

RICE AND POLENTA

# mushroom, pea and artichoke risotto

**preparation time** 15 minutes  **cooking time** 45 minutes  **serves** 4

3 cups (750ml) vegetable stock

2 cups (500ml) water

10g butter

1 tablespoon olive oil

1 medium brown onion (150g), chopped finely

2 cloves garlic, crushed

2 cups (400g) arborio rice

200g mushrooms, chopped coarsely

1 cup (250ml) dry white wine

¼ cup coarsely chopped fresh flat-leaf parsley

340g jar quartered marinated artichoke hearts, drained

1 cup (120g) frozen peas

⅔ cup (50g) coarsely grated parmesan

1 Place stock and the water in medium saucepan. Bring to a boil then reduce heat; simmer, covered.

2 Meanwhile, heat butter and oil in large saucepan; cook onion and garlic, stirring, until soft. Add rice and mushrooms; stir to coat in onion mixture. Stir in wine; cook, stirring, until wine is absorbed. Add ½ cup of the simmering stock mixture; cook, stirring, over low heat until stock is absorbed. Continue adding stock, in ½-cup batches, stirring, until stock is absorbed after each addition. Total cooking time should be about 35 minutes or until rice is tender.

3 Stir in remaining ingredients; cook, uncovered, until peas are tender.

PER SERVING  9.8g fat; 2358kJ (564 cal)

# cheesy pesto polenta

**preparation time** 10 minutes  **cooking time** 25 minutes  **serves** 4

2⅓ cups (580ml) water

2⅓ cups (580ml) milk

1 cup (170g) polenta

½ cup (40g) finely grated parmesan

30g butter, chopped

PESTO

2 tablespoons finely grated parmesan

2 tablespoons toasted pine nuts

2 tablespoons olive oil

1 clove garlic, crushed

1 cup firmly packed fresh basil leaves

1 Combine the water and milk in large saucepan; bring to a boil. Gradually sprinkle polenta over milk mixture; cook, stirring, until polenta thickens slightly.

2 Reduce heat; simmer, uncovered, about 20 minutes or until polenta is thickened, stirring occasionally.

3 Meanwhile, make pesto.

4 Stir cheese, butter and pesto into polenta.

PESTO  Blend or process ingredients until mixture forms a paste.

PER SERVING  31.3g fat; 2023kJ (483 cal)

# white wine risotto cakes with smoked chicken

**preparation time** 20 minutes  **cooking time** 45 minutes (plus cooling and refrigeration time)  **serves** 4

2¾ cups (680ml) chicken stock

10g butter

1 tablespoon olive oil

1 small brown onion (80g), chopped finely

1 clove garlic, crushed

⅔ cup (130g) arborio rice

¼ cup (60ml) dry white wine

¼ cup (20g) coarsely grated parmesan

2 tablespoons finely shredded fresh basil

1 tablespoon dijon mustard

1 tablespoon sour cream

2 tablespoons vegetable oil

32 baby rocket leaves

170g smoked chicken breast, shredded coarsely

1   Place stock in medium saucepan. Bring to a boil then reduce heat; simmer, covered.

2   Meanwhile, heat butter and half of the olive oil in medium saucepan; cook onion and garlic, stirring, until onion softens. Add rice; stir to coat in onion mixture. Add wine; cook, stirring, until wine is absorbed. Stir in ½ cup of the simmering stock; cook, stirring, over low heat until stock is absorbed. Continue adding stock, in ½-cup batches, stirring, until stock is absorbed after each addition. Total cooking time should be about 35 minutes or until rice is tender. Gently stir in cheese and basil; cool 20 minutes.

3   Divide risotto into four portions; using hands, shape portions into 1cm-deep patty-shaped cakes. Refrigerate, covered, 30 minutes.

4   Meanwhile, combine mustard and sour cream in small bowl.

5   Heat vegetable oil in large frying pan; cook risotto cakes, uncovered, until browned both sides and heated through.

6   Place each risotto cake on serving plate; top each with 8 rocket leaves, a quarter of the chicken then 2 teaspoons of the mustard mixture; drizzle with remaining olive oil.

**PER SERVING** 23.4g fat; 1676kJ (401 cal)

# creamy polenta with slow-roasted mushrooms

**preparation time** 20 minutes (plus standing time) **cooking time** 40 minutes **serves** 4

150g oyster mushrooms, halved

200g fresh shiitake mushrooms, halved

200g swiss brown mushrooms, halved

2 large flat mushrooms (350g), chopped coarsely

300g vine-ripened tomatoes, chopped coarsely

1 small red onion (100g), sliced thinly

2 cloves garlic, sliced thinly

1 tablespoon olive oil

10g dried porcini mushrooms

1 cup (250ml) boiling water

2 cups (500ml) milk

1 cup (250ml) cold water

¾ cup (125g) polenta

20g butter

⅓ cup (35g) finely grated parmesan

1 cup firmly packed fresh flat-leaf parsley leaves

½ cup coarsely chopped fresh chives

1   Preheat oven to slow (150°C/130°C fan-forced).

2   Combine oyster, shiitake, swiss brown and flat mushrooms, tomato, onion, garlic and oil in large baking dish; roast, uncovered, about 30 minutes or until mushrooms are tender.

3   Meanwhile, soak porcini in the boiling water in small jug for 15 minutes. Drain over small bowl; reserve liquid. Chop porcini finely.

4   Combine reserved liquid, milk and the cold water in medium saucepan; bring to a boil. Gradually add polenta to pan, stirring. Reduce heat; cook, stirring, about 5 minutes or until polenta thickens slightly. Stir in porcini, butter and cheese.

5   Stir herbs into mushroom mixture. Divide polenta among serving plates; top with mushroom mixture.

**PER SERVING**  17.8g fat; 1622kJ (388 cal)

# grilled herb polenta with semi-dried tomato and olive salad

**preparation time** 15 minutes (plus cooling and refrigeration time) **cooking time** 30 minutes **serves** 4

2 cups (500ml) water

2 cups (500ml) vegetable stock

1 cup (170g) polenta

⅓ cup (25g) finely grated parmesan

1 tablespoon finely chopped fresh flat-leaf parsley

1 tablespoon finely chopped fresh basil

SEMI-DRIED TOMATO AND OLIVE SALAD

100g baby cos lettuce, trimmed, leaves torn roughly

1⅓ cups (200g) drained semi-dried tomatoes

4 green onions, sliced thinly

¼ cup (50g) thinly sliced seeded black olives

SPICED MAYONNAISE

¾ cup (225g) mayonnaise

pinch cayenne pepper

¼ teaspoon ground cumin

¼ teaspoon ground coriander

¼ teaspoon ground turmeric

1 tablespoon lemon juice

1 Combine the water and stock in medium saucepan; bring to a boil. Gradually add polenta to liquid, stirring constantly. Reduce heat; cook, stirring, about 10 minutes or until polenta thickens. Stir in cheese, parsley and basil.

2 Spread polenta evenly into deep 19cm-square cake pan; cool 10 minutes. Cover; refrigerate about 3 hours or until firm.

3 Turn polenta onto board; trim edges. Cut into four squares; cut each square diagonally into two triangles. Cook polenta, in batches, on heated oiled grill plate (or grill or barbecue) until browned both sides.

4 Meanwhile, make semi-dried tomato and olive salad. Make spiced mayonnaise. Divide polenta among serving plates; top with salad, drizzle with spiced mayonnaise.

SEMI-DRIED TOMATO AND OLIVE SALAD  Combine ingredients in medium bowl.

SPICED MAYONNAISE  Whisk ingredients in small bowl until combined.

PER SERVING  25.7g fat; 2257kJ (539 cal)

# osso buco with semi-dried tomatoes and olives

**preparation time** 30 minutes  **cooking time** 2 hours 45 minutes  **serves** 6

12 pieces veal osso buco (3kg)

¼ cup (35g) plain flour

¼ cup (60ml) olive oil

40g butter

1 medium brown onion (150g), chopped coarsely

2 cloves garlic, chopped finely

3 trimmed celery stalks (300g), chopped coarsely

2 large carrots (360g), chopped coarsely

4 medium tomatoes (600g), chopped coarsely

2 tablespoons tomato paste

1 cup (250ml) dry white wine

1 cup (250ml) beef stock

400g can crushed tomatoes

4 sprigs fresh lemon thyme

½ cup (75g) drained semi-dried tomatoes

¼ cup (60ml) lemon juice

1 tablespoon finely grated lemon rind

½ cup (75g) seeded kalamata olives

GREMOLATA

1 tablespoon finely grated lemon rind

⅓ cup finely chopped fresh flat-leaf parsley

2 cloves garlic, chopped finely

1  Coat veal in flour; shake off excess. Heat oil in large deep saucepan; cook veal, in batches, until browned all over.

2  Melt butter in same pan; cook onion, garlic, celery and carrot, stirring, until vegetables just soften. Stir in fresh tomato, paste, wine, stock, undrained tomatoes and thyme. Return veal to pan, fitting pieces upright and tightly together in single layer. Bring to a boil then reduce heat; simmer, covered, 1¾ hours. Stir in semi-dried tomatoes; simmer, uncovered, about 30 minutes or until veal is tender.

3  Meanwhile, make gremolata.

4  Remove veal from pan; cover to keep warm. Bring sauce to a boil; boil, uncovered, about 10 minutes or until sauce thickens slightly. Stir in juice, rind and olives. Divide veal among serving plates; top with sauce, sprinkle with gremolata. Serve with soft polenta, if desired.

GREMOLATA  Combine ingredients in small bowl.

PER SERVING  20.5g fat; 2587kJ (619 cal)

MEAT AND POULTRY

# veal scaloppine with potato fennel gratin

**preparation time** 30 minutes  **cooking time** 1 hour 10 minutes  **serves** 4

400g potatoes

1 small fennel bulb (200g), sliced thinly

3 teaspoons plain flour

300ml cream

2 tablespoons milk

20g butter

⅓ cup (25g) coarsely grated parmesan

½ cup (35g) stale breadcrumbs

2 tablespoons olive oil

8 veal schnitzels (800g)

2 tablespoons lemon juice

¼ cup (60ml) dry white wine

1 clove garlic, crushed

¾ cup (180ml) chicken stock

1 teaspoon dijon mustard

2 tablespoons drained baby capers, rinsed

¼ cup coarsely chopped fresh flat-leaf parsley

1   Preheat oven to moderate (180°C/160°C fan-forced). Oil deep 1-litre (4-cup) baking dish.

2   Using sharp knife, mandoline or v-slicer, cut potatoes into very thin slices; pat dry with absorbent paper. Layer a third of the potato into prepared dish; top with half of the fennel. Continue layering remaining potato and fennel, finishing with potato.

3   Blend flour with a little of the cream in medium jug to form a smooth paste; stir in milk and remaining cream. Pour cream mixture over potato; dot with butter. Cover with foil; bake about 45 minutes or until vegetables are just tender. Remove foil, top with combined cheese and breadcrumbs; bake gratin, uncovered, about 20 minutes or until top is browned lightly.

4   Heat oil in large frying pan; cook veal, in batches, until cooked as desired. Cover to keep warm.

5   Add juice, wine and garlic to same pan. Bring to a boil then reduce heat; simmer, uncovered, until liquid is reduced by half. Add stock and mustard; simmer, uncovered, 5 minutes. Remove from heat; stir in capers and parsley. Serve veal topped with sauce and accompanied by gratin.

**PER SERVING**  48.7g fat; 3114kJ (745 cal)

# tuscan beef stew

**preparation time** 15 minutes  **cooking time** 2 hours 40 minutes  **serves** 4

1 tablespoon olive oil

400g spring onions, trimmed

1kg chuck steak, cut into 3cm cubes

30g butter

2 tablespoons plain flour

2 cups (500ml) dry red wine

1 cup (250ml) beef stock

1 cup (250ml) water

2 cloves garlic, crushed

6 sprigs thyme

2 bay leaves

1 trimmed celery stalk (75g), chopped coarsely

400g baby carrots, trimmed, halved

2 cups (250g) frozen peas

⅓ cup coarsely chopped fresh flat-leaf parsley

1  Heat oil in large heavy-based saucepan; cook onions, stirring occasionally, about 10 minutes or until browned lightly, remove from pan. Cook steak, in batches, over high heat in same pan, until browned all over.

2  Melt butter in same saucepan, add flour; cook, stirring, until mixture bubbles and thickens. Gradually stir in wine, stock and the water; stir until mixture boils and thickens. Return steak to pan with garlic, thyme and bay leaves. Bring to a boil then reduce heat; simmer, covered, 1½ hours.

3  Add onion to pan with celery and carrot; simmer, covered, 30 minutes. Add peas; simmer, uncovered, until peas are just tender. Stir in parsley just before serving. Serve with penne or farfalle, if desired.

**PER SERVING**  22.9g fat; 2500kJ (597 cal)

# saltimbocca with risotto milanese

**preparation time** 10 minutes  **cooking time** 25 minutes  **serves** 4

*Saltimbocca is a classic Italian veal dish that literally means "jump in the mouth" – just the sensation the wonderful flavours will produce with your first bite. Tinged with the taste and colour of saffron, a milanese is the classic risotto generally served with saltimbocca.*

8 veal steaks (680g)

4 slices prosciutto (60g), halved crossways

8 fresh sage leaves

½ cup (50g) finely grated pecorino

40g butter

1 cup (250ml) dry white wine

1 tablespoon coarsely chopped fresh sage

RISOTTO MILANESE

1½ cups (375ml) water

2 cups (500ml) chicken stock

½ cup (125ml) dry white wine

¼ teaspoon saffron threads

20g butter

1 large brown onion (200g), chopped finely

2 cups (400g) arborio rice

¼ cup (20g) finely grated parmesan

1   Place steaks on board. Place one piece prosciutto, one sage leaf and an eighth of the cheese on each steak; fold in half to encase filling, secure with a toothpick or small skewer.

2   Make risotto milanese.

3   Melt half of the butter in medium frying pan; cook saltimbocca, in batches, about 5 minutes or until browned both sides and cooked through. Cover to keep warm.

4   Pour wine into same frying pan; bring to a boil. Boil, uncovered, until wine is reduced by half. Stir in remaining butter then chopped sage.

5   Divide risotto milanese and saltimbocca among serving plates; drizzle saltimbocca with sauce and accompany with steamed green beans, if desired.

RISOTTO MILANESE  Place the water, stock, wine and saffron in medium saucepan. Bring to a boil then reduce heat; simmer, covered. Heat butter in another medium saucepan; cook onion, stirring, until onion softens. Add rice, stir to coat in onion mixture. Stir in ½ cup of the simmering stock mixture; cook, stirring, over low heat, until stock is absorbed. Continue adding stock mixture, in ½-cup batches, stirring, until absorbed after each addition. Total cooking time should be about 35 minutes or until rice is just tender. Gently stir cheese into risotto.

**PER SERVING**  23.3g fat; 3429kJ (819 cal)

# venetian calves liver and onions

*A traditional Venetian dish, the classic fegato alla veneziana is found on the menus of Italian restaurants around the world yet it is easy enough to make at home. The secret to success is that the calves liver should be sliced into paper-thin scallops then quickly seared. Overcooking will toughen its delicate texture.*

2 cups (500ml) water

2 cups (500ml) milk

1 cup (170g) polenta

½ cup (40g) finely grated parmesan

½ cup (125ml) cream

¼ cup coarsely chopped fresh flat-leaf parsley

40g butter

2 tablespoons olive oil

3 medium brown onions (450g), sliced thinly

2 teaspoons cornflour

¾ cup (180ml) beef stock

2 teaspoons dijon mustard

500g calves liver, sliced thinly

½ teaspoon balsamic vinegar

1   Combine the water and milk in large saucepan; bring to a boil. Add polenta in a slow, steady stream, stirring constantlly. Reduce heat; simmer, stirring occasionally, about 20 minutes or until polenta thickens. Stir in cheese, cream and parsley. Cover to keep warm.

2   Meanwhile, heat butter and half of the oil in large frying pan; cook onion, stirring, until onion softens. Stir in blended cornflour, stock and mustard; cook, stirring, until sauce boils and thickens.

3   Heat remaining oil in large frying pan; cook liver quickly over high heat until browned both sides and cooked as desired.

4   Stir vinegar into sauce just before serving with polenta and liver; accompany with a balsamic-dressed mixed green salad, if desired.

PER SERVING  47.2g fat; 3171kJ (757 cal)

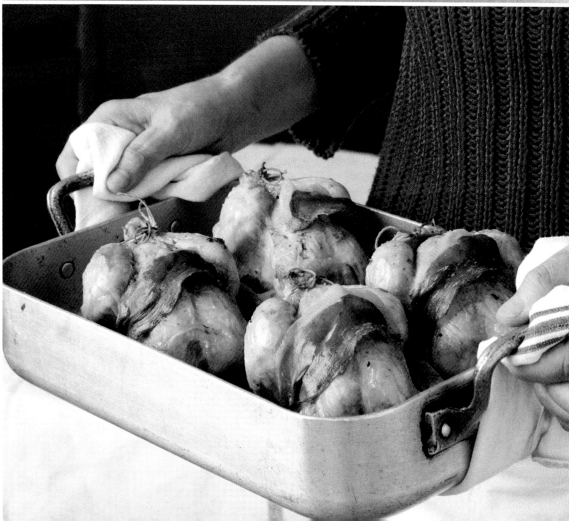

# lamb with white wine and mascarpone sauce

**preparation time** 10 minutes  **cooking time** 15 minutes  **serves** 4

¼ cup (60ml) olive oil

12 fresh sage leaves

100g sliced prosciutto

8 lamb steaks (640g)

1 clove garlic, crushed

¾ cup (180ml) dry white wine

½ cup (120g) mascarpone

¼ cup (60ml) cream

1  Heat oil in medium frying pan; cook sage until crisp. Drain on absorbent paper. Cook prosciutto, stirring, until crisp; drain on absorbent paper.

2  Cook lamb in same pan until browned both sides and cooked as desired. Remove from pan.

3  Cook garlic in same pan, stirring, until fragrant; add wine. Bring to a boil then reduce heat; simmer, uncovered, until liquid reduces by half. Add mascarpone and cream; cook, stirring, over heat until sauce boils and thickens slightly.

4  Divide lamb among serving plates; top with prosciutto and sage, drizzle with sauce. Serve with steamed asparagus, if desired.

**PER SERVING**  49.9g fat; 2650kJ (633 cal)

# prosciutto-wrapped spatchcocks with lemon and sage

**preparation time** 20 minutes  **cooking time** 45 minutes  **serves** 8

8 x 400g spatchcocks

1 medium lemon (140g)

16 fresh sage leaves

8 thin slices prosciutto (120g)

2 medium lemons (280g), extra

FENNEL RUB

1 teaspoon toasted fennel seeds, crushed

1 clove garlic, crushed

2 tablespoons olive oil

Salt and freshly ground black pepper

1  Preheat oven to hot (220°C/200°C fan-forced). Make fennel rub.

2  Wash the spatchcocks under cold water; clean cavity well. Pat dry inside and out with absorbent paper.

3  Cut lemon into eight wedges. Place a wedge and 2 sage leaves into each spatchcock cavity. Rub fennel mixture all over spatchcocks. Wrap a slice of prosciutto around the middle of each spatchcock; secure with toothpick.

4  Divide spatchcocks between two baking dishes. Roast, uncovered, about 45 minutes or until browned and cooked through. Serve spatchcocks with extra lemon wedges, if desired.

FENNEL RUB  Combine ingredients in a small bowl.

**PER SERVING**  37.1g fat 2140kJ (512 cal)

# veal with artichokes, olives and lemon

preparation time 40 minutes  cooking time 2 hours 25 minutes  serves 6

1 medium unpeeled lemon (140g), chopped coarsely

4 medium globe artichokes (800g)

1.2kg diced veal neck

¼ cup (35g) plain flour

50g butter

¼ cup (60ml) olive oil

1 medium brown onion (150g), chopped finely

1 medium carrot (120g), chopped finely

2 cloves garlic, chopped finely

2 sprigs fresh marjoram

2 sprigs fresh oregano

1 cup (250ml) dry white wine

2 cups (500ml) chicken stock

1 cup (150g) seeded kalamata olives

2 teaspoons finely grated lemon rind

2 tablespoons lemon juice

2 tablespoons fresh oregano leaves

1 medium lemon (140g), cut into 6 wedges

1  Place chopped lemon in large bowl half-filled with cold water. Discard outer leaves from artichokes; cut tips from remaining leaves. Trim then peel stalks. Quarter artichokes lengthways; using teaspoon, remove and discard chokes. Place in lemon water.

2  Preheat oven to moderately slow (170°C/150°C fan-forced).

3  Coat veal in flour; shake off excess. Heat butter and 2 tablespoons of the oil in large flameproof casserole dish; cook veal, in batches, until browned all over.

4  Heat remaining oil in same dish; cook onion, carrot, garlic, marjoram and oregano sprigs, stirring, until vegetables soften. Add wine; bring to a boil. Return veal to dish with stock, cover; cook in oven 1 hour.

5  Add artichokes; cook in oven 30 minutes. Uncover; cook a further 30 minutes or until veal is tender. Stir in olives, rind and juice. Divide among serving plates; top with oregano leaves. Serve with lemon wedges and penne, if desired.

PER SERVING  21.6g fat; 2040kJ (488 cal)

# braised pork with pancetta and fennel

**preparation time** 25 minutes  **cooking time** 2 hours 50 minutes  **serves** 6

2 tablespoons olive oil

1.5kg pork shoulder, rolled and tied

2 cloves garlic, crushed

1 medium brown onion (150g), chopped coarsely

½ small fennel bulb (100g), chopped coarsely

8 slices hot pancetta (120g), chopped coarsely

1 tablespoon tomato paste

½ cup (125ml) dry white wine

400g can whole tomatoes

1 cup (250ml) chicken stock

1 cup (250ml) water

2 sprigs fresh rosemary

2 large fennel bulbs (1kg), halved, sliced thickly

SPICE RUB

1 teaspoon fennel seeds

2 teaspoons dried oregano

½ teaspoon cayenne pepper

1 tablespoon cracked black pepper

1 tablespoon sea salt

2 teaspoons olive oil

1  Preheat oven to moderate (180°C/160°C fan-forced).

2  Heat oil in large flameproof casserole dish; cook pork, uncovered, until browned all over.

3  Meanwhile, make spice rub.

4  Remove pork from dish; discard all but 1 tablespoon of the oil in dish. Cook garlic, onion, chopped fennel and pancetta in same dish, stirring, until onion softens. Add paste; cook, stirring, 2 minutes.

5  Rub pork with spice rub. Return pork to dish with wine, undrained tomatoes, stock, the water and rosemary; bring to a boil. Cover; cook in oven 1 hour.

6  Add sliced fennel; cook, covered, in oven 1 hour. Remove pork from dish; discard rind. Cover to keep warm.

7  Meanwhile, cook braising liquid in dish over medium heat, uncovered, until thickened slightly. Return sliced pork to dish; serve pork and sauce with warm Italian bread, if desired.

SPICE RUB  Combine ingredients in a small bowl.

TIP  Ask your butcher to roll and tie the pork shoulder for you.

PER SERVING  28g fat; 2525 kJ (604 cal)

# chicken cacciatore with split pea salad

preparation time 20 minutes (plus standing time)  cooking time 2 hours 10 minutes  serves 4

1 cup (200g) green split peas

2 tablespoons olive oil

1.5kg chicken pieces, skin on

1 medium brown onion (150g), chopped finely

½ cup (125ml) dry white wine

2 tablespoons white wine vinegar

½ cup (125ml) chicken stock

410g can crushed tomatoes

¼ cup (70g) tomato paste

½ cup (60g) seeded black olives, chopped coarsely

2 tablespoons drained capers, rinsed, chopped coarsely

2 cloves garlic, crushed

½ cup coarsely chopped fresh flat-leaf parsley

½ cup coarsely chopped fresh basil

1   Place peas in medium bowl, cover with cold water; stand overnight, drain. Rinse under cold water; drain.

2   Heat half of the oil in large deep saucepan; cook chicken, in batches, until browned all over.

3   Cook onion in same pan, stirring, until onion softens. Stir in wine, vinegar, stock, undrained tomatoes and paste.

4   Return chicken to pan, fitting pieces upright and tightly together in single layer. Bring to a boil then reduce heat; simmer, covered, 1 hour. Uncover; simmer about 45 minutes or until chicken is tender. Skim fat from surface; stir in olives.

5   Meanwhile, place peas in large saucepan of boiling water. Return to a boil then reduce heat; simmer, uncovered, about 40 minutes or until peas are tender, drain.

6   Combine peas, capers, garlic, herbs and remaining oil in large bowl. Serve chicken cacciatore with split pea salad.

PER SERVING  37.2g fat; 2830kJ (677 cal)

# chicken stuffed with ricotta, basil and prosciutto

**preparation time** 30 minutes  **cooking time** 2 hours  **serves** 4

8 chicken thigh cutlets (1.3kg)

⅔ cup (130g) ricotta

4 slices prosciutto (60g), halved lengthways

8 large fresh basil leaves

1 tablespoon olive oil

1 medium brown onion (150g), chopped finely

1 medium carrot (120g), chopped finely

1 trimmed celery stalk (100g), chopped finely

2 cloves garlic, chopped finely

2 tablespoons tomato paste

½ cup (125ml) dry white wine

8 small tomatoes (720g), peeled, chopped coarsely

425g can diced tomatoes

½ cup (125ml) water

1  Preheat oven to moderately slow (170°C/150°C fan-forced).

2  Using small sharp knife, cut a pocket through thickest part of each cutlet over the bone, push 1 tablespoon of the cheese, one slice of prosciutto and one basil leaf into each pocket; secure pocket closed with toothpick.

3  Heat oil in large deep flameproof baking dish; cook chicken, in batches, until browned all over.

4  Cook onion, carrot, celery and garlic in same dish, stirring, about 5 minutes or until onion softens. Add paste; cook, stirring, 2 minutes. Add wine. Bring to a boil then reduce heat; simmer, uncovered, 1 minute. Add chopped tomato, undrained diced tomatoes and the water. Bring to a boil then reduce heat; simmer, uncovered, 10 minutes.

5  Return chicken to dish, cover; cook 1 hour. Uncover; cook a further 20 minutes or until chicken is cooked through. Remove toothpicks; serve chicken with sourdough bread, if desired.

**PER SERVING**  46.8g fat; 2922kJ (699 cal)

# kingfish with salsa verde and white bean puree

**preparation time** 30 minutes  **cooking time** 25 minutes  **serves** 4

1 tablespoon olive oil

1 clove garlic, crushed

1 medium brown onion (150g), chopped finely

3 x 400g cans white beans, rinsed, drained

1 cup (250ml) chicken stock

¼ cup (60ml) cream

4 kingfish fillets (800g), skin on

SALSA VERDE

½ cup finely chopped fresh flat-leaf parsley

¼ cup finely chopped fresh mint

¼ cup finely chopped fresh dill

¼ cup finely chopped fresh chives

1 tablespoon wholegrain mustard

2 tablespoons lemon juice

2 tablespoons drained baby capers, rinsed, chopped finely

1 clove garlic, crushed

¼ cup (60ml) olive oil

1   Make salsa verde.

2   Heat oil in medium saucepan; cook garlic and onion, stirring, until onion softens. Add beans and stock. Bring to a boil then reduce heat; simmer, uncovered, until almost all liquid has evaporated. Stir in cream; blend or process bean mixture until smooth.

3   Meanwhile, cook fish, skin-side down, in large heated oiled frying pan until cooked as desired.

4   Serve fish on white bean puree, topped with salsa verde.

SALSA VERDE  Combine ingredients in a small bowl.

TIP  Can be replaced with any firm white fish.

PER SERVING  23.5g fat; 1789kJ (428 cal)

SEAFOOD

# octopus braised in red wine

**preparation time** 15 minutes  **cooking time** 1 hour 45 minutes  **serves** 6

⅓ cup (80ml) olive oil

600g baby onions, halved

4 cloves garlic, crushed

1.5kg cleaned baby octopus, halved

1½ cups (375ml) dry red wine

⅓ cup (95g) tomato paste

⅓ cup (80ml) red wine vinegar

3 large tomatoes (660g), peeled, seeded, chopped coarsely

2 bay leaves

1 fresh long red chilli, chopped finely

10 drained anchovy fillets (30g), chopped coarsely

⅓ cup finely chopped fresh oregano

1 cup coarsely chopped fresh flat-leaf parsley

1  Heat oil in large saucepan; cook onion and garlic, stirring, until onion softens. Add octopus; cook, stirring, until just changed in colour.

2  Add wine; cook, stirring, about 5 minutes or until pan liquid is reduced by about a third. Add tomato paste, vinegar, tomato, bay leaves, chilli and anchovies. Bring to a boil then reduce heat; simmer, covered, 1 hour. Uncover; simmer about 30 minutes or until sauce thickens and octopus is tender.

3  Remove from heat, stir in oregano and parsley; serve with thick slices of toasted ciabatta, if desired.

TIP  Ask your fishmonger to clean the octopus and remove their beaks.

**PER SERVING** 17.5g fat; 2145kJ (512 cal)

# char-grilled squid, rocket and parmesan salad

preparation time 20 minutes **cooking time** 10 minutes  **serves** 4

1kg squid hoods

2 tablespoons olive oil

1 tablespoon finely grated lemon rind

⅓ cup (80ml) lemon juice

1 clove garlic, crushed

150g rocket

150g semi-dried tomatoes, drained, chopped coarsely

1 small red onion (100g), sliced thinly

1 tablespoon drained baby capers, rinsed

80g parmesan, shaved

2 tablespoons balsamic vinegar

2 tablespoons olive oil, extra

1   Halve squid lengthways, score insides in crosshatch pattern then cut into 5cm strips. Combine squid in medium bowl with oil, rind, juice and garlic, cover; refrigerate 10 minutes.

2   Meanwhile, combine rocket, tomato, onion, capers and cheese in large bowl.

3   Drain squid; discard marinade. Cook squid in batches, on heated oiled grill plate (or grill or barbecue) until browned and cooked through.

4   Add squid to salad with combined vinegar and extra oil; toss to combine.

PER SERVING  41.3g fat; 2750kJ (657 cal)

# slow-roasted pesto salmon

**preparation time** 20 minutes **cooking time** 45 minutes **serves** 8

1 cup loosely packed fresh basil leaves

2 cloves garlic, chopped coarsely

2 tablespoons toasted pine nuts

2 tablespoons lemon juice

¼ cup (60ml) olive oil

1.5kg piece salmon fillet, skin on

2 tablespoons olive oil, extra

2 large red capsicums (700g), chopped coarsely

1 large red onion (300g), chopped coarsely

1 Preheat oven to moderately slow (170°C/150°C fan-forced).

2 Blend or process basil, garlic, pine nuts and juice until combined. With motor operating, gradually add oil in thin, steady stream until pesto thickens slightly.

3 Place fish, skin-side down, on piece of lightly oiled foil large enough to completely enclose fish; coat fish with half of the pesto. Gather corners of foil together above fish; twist to enclose securely. Place parcel on oven tray; roast about 45 minutes or until cooked as desired.

4 Meanwhile, heat extra oil in large frying pan; cook capsicum and onion, stirring, until onion softens.

5 Place fish parcel on serving platter, unwrap; top with onion mixture, drizzle with remaining pesto. Serve with rocket, if desired.

TIP If the pesto is a little too thick for your liking, thin it down with a little olive oil before drizzling over the salmon.

**PER SERVING** 27.5g fat; 1802kJ (431 cal)

# pan-fried fish fillets with pancetta and caper herb butter

**preparation time** 15 minutes  **cooking time** 10 minutes  **serves** 4

80g butter, softened

2 tablespoons coarsely chopped fresh flat-leaf parsley

1 tablespoon capers, rinsed, drained

2 cloves garlic, quartered

2 green onions, chopped coarsely

8 slices pancetta (120g)

4 white fish fillets (600g)

1 tablespoon olive oil

350g asparagus, trimmed

1 Blend or process butter, parsley, capers, garlic and onion until mixture forms a smooth paste.

2 Spread 1 heaped tablespoon of the butter mixture and two slices of the pancetta on each fish fillet.

3 Heat oil in large heavy-based frying pan; cook fish, pancetta-side down, until pancetta is crisp. Turn fish carefully; cook, uncovered, until cooked as desired.

4 Meanwhile, boil, steam or microwave asparagus until tender.

5 Drizzle fish with pan juices, serve with asparagus.

**PER SERVING**  28.5g fat; 1731kJ (414 cal)

# anchovy and garlic tuna with tomato and oregano

**preparation time** 20 minutes **cooking time** 25 minutes **serves** 4

1kg tuna fillet, trimmed, skinned

3 cloves garlic, sliced thinly

¼ cup firmly packed fresh oregano leaves

8 drained anchovy fillets, halved

¼ cup (60ml) olive oil

1 large brown onion (200g), sliced thinly

4 large egg tomatoes (360g), seeded, chopped coarsely

¼ cup (60ml) balsamic vinegar

2 tablespoons dry white wine

¼ cup (60ml) fish stock

1 tablespoon drained baby capers, rinsed

¼ cup coarsely chopped fresh basil

1   Preheat oven to moderately hot (200°C/180°C fan-forced).
2   Using sharp knife, make 16 cuts in tuna; press 16 slices of the garlic, 16 oregano leaves and anchovy halves into cuts. Reserve remaining garlic and oregano.
3   Heat 2 tablespoons of the oil in medium deep flameproof baking dish; cook tuna, uncovered, until browned. Remove from dish.
4   Heat remaining oil in same dish; cook onion, stirring, until soft. Combine tomato, vinegar, wine, stock, remaining garlic and remaining oregano in dish then add tuna; bring to a boil. Cook, uncovered, about 10 minutes or until tuna is cooked as desired. Remove tuna from dish; slice thinly. Stir capers and basil into sauce in dish.
5   Serve tuna with sauce and mash, if desired.

**PER SERVING** 28.8g fat; 2312kJ (553 cal)

# cioppino

preparation time 30 minutes  **cooking time** 40 minutes **serves** 4

2 teaspoons olive oil

1 medium brown onion (150g), chopped coarsely

1 baby fennel bulb (130g), trimmed, chopped coarsely

3 cloves garlic, crushed

6 medium tomatoes (1kg), chopped coarsely

425g can crushed tomatoes

½ cup (125ml) dry white wine

1½ cups (375ml) fish stock

2 cooked blue swimmer crabs (700g)

500g uncooked large king prawns

450g swordfish steaks

400g clams, rinsed

150g scallops

¼ cup coarsely chopped fresh basil

½ cup coarsely chopped fresh flat-leaf parsley

1 Heat oil in large saucepan; cook onion, fennel and garlic, stirring, until onion softens. Add fresh tomato; cook, stirring, about 5 minutes or until pulpy. Stir in undrained crushed tomatoes, wine and stock; reduce heat, simmer, covered, 20 minutes.

2 Meanwhile, remove back shell from crabs; discard grey gills. Rinse crab; using sharp knife, chop each crab into four pieces. Shell and devein prawns, leaving tails intact. Chop fish into 2cm pieces.

3 Add clams to pan; simmer, covered, about 5 minutes or until clams open (discard any that do not). Add remaining seafood; cook, stirring occasionally, about 5 minutes or until seafood has changed in colour and is cooked as desired. Remove from heat; stir in herbs.

TIP Serve with a warm French bread stick.

PER SERVING 6.4g fat; 1476kJ (352 cal)

80

# swordfish with celery and bean salad

**preparation time** 15 minutes  **cooking time** 5 minutes  **serves** 4

⅓ cup (80ml) lemon juice

2 cloves garlic, chopped finely

¼ teaspoon salt

¼ teaspoon cracked black pepper

⅓ cup (80ml) extra virgin olive oil

1 tablespoon fresh oregano leaves, torn

1 tablespoon baby capers, rinsed, drained

4 swordfish steaks (700g)

CELERY AND BEAN SALAD

2 trimmed celery stalks (200g), halved, sliced thinly

300g can cannellini beans, rinsed, drained

¼ cup coarsely chopped young celery leaves

1   Combine juice, garlic, salt, pepper and oil in medium bowl; whisk until thickened slightly. Stir in oregano and capers.

2   Heat lightly oiled, large frying pan; cook fish until cooked as desired. Remove from pan.

3   Add half of the dressing to same pan, bring to a boil.

4   Serve fish with celery and bean salad, drizzled with warm dressing.

CELERY AND BEAN SALAD  Combine ingredients in small bowl. Add remaining dressing; toss gently.

TIP  Swordfish can be replaced with any firm white fish.

PER SERVING  22.3g fat; 1542kJ (369 cal)

# tuscan white bean salad

**preparation time** 20 minutes  **serves** 4

*Many varieties of already cooked white beans are available canned, among them cannellini, butter and haricot beans; any of these are suitable for use in this salad.*

2 x 400g cans white beans, rinsed, drained

1 medium red onion (170g), chopped finely

⅔ cup (100g) drained semi-dried tomatoes

150g mozzarella, cut into 1cm pieces

½ cup (75g) seeded kalamata olives

150g rocket

OREGANO BALSAMIC VINAIGRETTE

1 clove garlic, crushed

1 tablespoon finely chopped fresh oregano

¼ cup (60ml) balsamic vinegar

¼ cup (60ml) extra virgin olive oil

1 Combine beans, onion, tomato, cheese and olives in medium bowl.

2 Make oregano balsamic vinaigrette.

3 Drizzle salad with vinaigrette; toss to combine. Serve salad with rocket.

OREGANO BALSAMIC VINAIGRETTE  Combine all the ingredients in a screw-top jar; shake well.

PER SERVING  16.4g fat; 1056kJ (252 cal)

TRADITIONAL ITALIAN

SALADS AND VEGETABLES

# panzanella

**preparation time** 15 minutes  **cooking time** 10 minutes  **serves** 4

*This Italian bread salad was originally created as a way of using up stale bread – but our version, made with fresh wood-fired ciabatta, is even more delicious.*

½ long loaf ciabatta (250g)

1 clove garlic, crushed

¼ cup (60ml) olive oil

500g cherry tomatoes, halved

1 lebanese cucumber (130g), seeded, sliced thinly

1 medium avocado (250g), chopped coarsely

¼ cup (50g) drained capers, rinsed

1 large yellow capsicum (350g), chopped coarsely

2 x 400g cans white beans, rinsed, drained

½ cup coarsely chopped fresh basil

TOMATO VINAIGRETTE

½ cup (125ml) tomato juice

¼ cup (60ml) red wine vinegar

⅓ cup (80ml) olive oil

1  Preheat oven to moderately hot (200°C/180°C fan-forced).

2  Cut bread into 2cm cubes. Combine bread in large bowl with combined garlic and oil; toss to coat bread in oil mixture. Place bread, in single layer, on oven tray; bake about 10 minutes or until browned lightly.

3  Meanwhile, make tomato vinaigrette.

4  Place bread in same large bowl with remaining ingredients and vinaigrette; toss gently to combine.

TOMATO VINAIGRETTE  Combine ingredients in screw-top jar; shake well.

TIP  Ciabatta is readily available from most supermarkets; however, any crisp-crusted Italian bread can be used in this recipe.

PER SERVING  45.8g fat; 2556kJ (611 cal)

# tiella

**preparation time** 30 minutes (plus standing time) **cooking time** 1 hour 30 minutes **serves** 8

*From the Apulia region in the south-east of Italy, a tiella is both a homely recipe made with eggplant and potatoes and the name of the dish in which it is traditionally cooked.*

2 small eggplants (460g)

2 tablespoons coarse cooking salt

1kg medium tomatoes, peeled, seeded, chopped finely

1 medium brown onion (150g), chopped finely

2 trimmed celery stalks (150g), chopped finely

2 cloves garlic, crushed

1 tablespoon finely chopped fresh oregano

1 tablespoon finely chopped fresh flat-leaf parsley

1kg sebago potatoes, peeled

¼ cup (60ml) olive oil

2 tablespoons fresh oregano leaves

1   Cut eggplants into thin slices, sprinkle with salt; stand in colander in sink or over large bowl 30 minutes. Rinse eggplant well under cold water; pat dry with absorbent paper.

2   Preheat oven to moderate (180°C/160°C fan-forced).

3   Combine tomato, onion, celery, garlic, chopped oregano and parsley in medium bowl.

4   Using sharp knife, mandoline or v-slicer, cut potatoes into thin slices; pat dry with absorbent paper. Place half of the potato in lightly oiled shallow 2-litre (8-cup) baking dish; top with half of the eggplant, half of the tomato mixture, then drizzle with half of the oil. Repeat layering with remaining potato, eggplant, tomato mixture and oil.

5   Cover dish with foil; bake 1 hour. Remove foil; bake a further 30 minutes or until vegetables are tender. Sprinkle tiella with oregano leaves.

**PER SERVING**  7.6g fat; 675kJ (161 cal)

# caprese salad

**preparation time** 15 minutes  **serves** 4

3 large egg tomatoes (270g), sliced thinly

5 bocconcini (300g), sliced thinly

2 tablespoons olive oil

⅓ cup loosely packed fresh basil leaves

1   Arrange tomato and cheese alternately on serving platter.

2   Drizzle with oil; sprinkle with basil, and salt and pepper, if desired.

**PER SERVING**  20.6g fat; 1007kJ (241 cal)

# baby zucchini with garlic crumbs

**preparation time** 15 minutes  **cooking time** 15 minutes  **serves** 8

2 tablespoons extra virgin olive oil

40g butter

2 thick slices ciabatta (50g), crusts removed, chopped finely in cubes

2 cloves garlic, crushed

1 tablespoon toasted pine nuts, chopped coarsely

1 teaspoon finely grated lemon rind

2 tablespoons chopped fresh flat-leaf parsley

1 tablespoon dried currants

24 small zucchini flowers (700g)

1   Heat half the oil and butter in large frying pan; add bread cubes, cook, stirring, until browned lightly. Add garlic, cook until fragrant. Stir in pine nuts, rind, parsley and currants. Remove from pan; cover to keep warm.

2   Heat the remaining oil and butter in same frying pan; add zucchini, cook, covered loosely, until browned lightly and just tender.

3   Serve the zucchini sprinkled with bread mixture.

TIP   If zucchini flowers are not available, substitute small zucchini quartered lengthways.

**PER SERVING**  10.5g fat; 535kJ (128 cal)

# char-grilled vegetable stack with basil sauce

**preparation time** 35 minutes  **cooking time** 35 minutes  **serves** 4

4 large red capsicums (1.4kg)

4 flat mushrooms (320g)

6 baby eggplants (360g), halved lengthways

150g mesclun

14 bocconcini (420g), sliced thickly

LEMON OIL

2 tablespoons lemon juice

2 tablespoons olive oil

1 teaspoon finely grated lemon rind

BASIL DRESSING

1 cup firmly packed fresh basil leaves

1 tablespoon wholegrain mustard

2 tablespoons red wine vinegar

1 tablespoon water

¼ cup (60ml) olive oil

1   Make lemon oil. Make basil dressing.

2   Quarter capsicums; discard seeds and membranes. Roast under grill or in very hot oven, skin-side up, until skin blisters and blackens. Cover capsicum pieces with plastic wrap or paper for 5 minutes; peel away skin then cut into thick slices.

3   Meanwhile, cook mushrooms and eggplant, in batches, on heated oiled grill plate (or grill or barbecue) until browned all over.

4   Place mesclun in large bowl; drizzle with lemon oil, toss to combine.

5   Divide mesclun, mushrooms, eggplant, cheese and capsicum among serving plates; drizzle with basil dressing.

LEMON OIL   Combine ingredients in screw-top jar; shake well.

BASIL DRESSING   Blend or process ingredients until smooth.

**PER SERVING**  40.2g fat; 2294kJ (548 cal)

# napoletana pizza

**preparation time** 20 minutes (plus standing time)  **cooking time** 30 minutes  **serves** 6

300g mozzarella, sliced thinly

¼ cup coarsely torn basil

**BASIC PIZZA DOUGH**

2 teaspoons (7g) instant yeast

½ teaspoon salt

2½ cups (375g) plain flour

1 cup (250ml) warm water

1 tablespoon olive oil

**BASIC TOMATO PIZZA SAUCE**

1 tablespoon olive oil

1 small white onion (80g), chopped finely

2 cloves garlic, crushed

425g canned tomatoes

¼ cup (70g) tomato paste

1 teaspoon white sugar

1 tablespoon fresh oregano

1  Make pizza dough and tomato pizza sauce.

2  Preheat oven to moderately hot (200°C/180°C fan-forced).

3  Halve basic pizza dough; roll each half on lightly floured surface to form 30cm round. Place on two oiled pizza trays. Spread each with half of the basic tomato pizza sauce; top with cheese.

4  Bake, uncovered, about 15 minutes or until crust is golden and cheese is bubbling. Sprinkle each with basil before serving.

**BASIC PIZZA DOUGH**  Combine yeast, salt and sifted flour in large bowl; mix well. Gradually stir in combined water and oil. Knead on well-floured surface for about 10 minutes or until smooth and elastic. Place dough in large oiled bowl; cover, stand in warm place about 30 minutes or until dough doubles in size. Punch down dough with fist; knead dough on lightly floured surface until smooth. Roll out dough as required.

**BASIC TOMATO PIZZA SAUCE**  Heat oil in medium frying pan; cook onion, stirring over low heat, until soft. Stir in garlic and undrained, crushed tomatoes, paste, sugar and oregano. Simmer, uncovered, about 15 minutes or until mixture thickens.

**TIPS**  Purchased pizza bases can be used in place of the basic pizza dough. Tomato pizza sauce can be made up to two days ahead; store in the refrigerator.

**PER SERVING**  18.1g fat; 1890kJ (452 cal)

# onion, anchovy and olive pizzetta

**preparation time** 15 minutes  **cooking time** 20 minutes  **serves** 4

1 tablespoon olive oil

3 medium brown onions (450g), sliced thinly

2 tablespoons dry sherry

1 quantity basic pizza dough (see page 92)

2 tablespoons tomato paste

12 drained anchovy fillets, chopped coarsely

¼ cup (40g) thinly sliced seeded kalamata olives

2 tablespoons fresh oregano leaves

1   Heat oil in large frying pan; cook onion, stirring, until browned lightly. Add sherry; cook, stirring, until sherry evaporates.

2   Preheat grill plate (or grill or barbecue) to medium heat.

3   Divide pizza dough into four portions; roll each portion, on lightly floured surface, to form 15cm-round pizzetta base. Cover grill plate with double thickness of oiled foil. Place pizzetta bases on foil; cook, uncovered, 5 minutes.

4   Using metal tongs, turn bases; spread cooked sides with tomato paste. Divide onion mixture among pizzetta; top with anchovies, olives and oregano. Cook, covered, over low heat about 5 minutes or until bases are cooked through.

**PER SERVING** 6.8g fat; 1835kJ (439 cal)

# fig, prosciutto and goat cheese pizzetta

**preparation time** 10 minutes  **cooking time** 10 minutes  **serves** 4

1 quantity basic pizza dough (see page 92)

⅓ cup (85g) bottled tomato pasta sauce

100g goat cheese, crumbled

2 large figs (160g), cut into thin wedges

4 slices prosciutto (60g), chopped coarsely

25g baby rocket leaves

1  Preheat oven to moderately hot (200°C/180°C fan-forced).

2  Divide pizza dough into four portions; roll each portion, on lightly floured surface, to form 15cm-round pizzetta base. Place pizzetta bases on two oven trays.

3  Spread bases with pasta sauce. Divide cheese, fig and prosciutto among bases. Cook about 10 minutes or until bases are cooked through; top with rocket.

**PER SERVING**  6.4g fat; 1797kJ (430 cal)

# potato and rosemary pizza

**preparation time** 25 minutes (plus standing time) **cooking time** 15 minutes **serves** 4

2 teaspoons (7g) dry yeast

½ teaspoon caster sugar

¾ cup (180ml) warm water

2 cups (300g) plain flour

1 teaspoon salt

2 tablespoons extra virgin olive oil

2 tablespoons polenta

4 small potatoes (480g), sliced thinly

2 tablespoons fresh rosemary

2 cloves garlic, crushed

1 tablespoon extra virgin olive oil, extra

1 Combine yeast, sugar and the water in small bowl; cover, stand in a warm place about 10 minutes or until frothy.

2 Sift flour and salt into large bowl. Stir in yeast mixture and olive oil; mix to a soft dough. Bring dough together with hands; add a little extra water if necessary.

3 Knead dough on lightly floured surface about 10 minutes or until smooth and elastic. Place dough in large oiled bowl; cover, stand in warm place about 30 minutes or until dough doubles in size.

4 Preheat oven to very hot (250°C/230°C fan-forced).

5 Punch dough down with fist; knead dough on lightly floured surface until smooth. Divide dough in half. Roll each half to form a 20cm x 35cm rectangle, place on oiled rectangular trays. Sprinkle with polenta; prick bases with a fork.

6 Layer potato, overlapping slightly, over top of pizza. Sprinkle with rosemary, drizzle with combined garlic and extra oil.

7 Cook on lowest shelf in oven about 15 minutes or until base and potato are browned and crisp. Sprinkle with salt before serving, if desired.

**PER SERVING** 14.8g fat; 1926kJ (460 cal)

# sicilian stuffed pizza

**preparation time** 30 minutes (plus standing time) **cooking time** 35 minutes (plus standing time) **serves** 4

*Variously called sfinciuni or sfincione in Sicily, we call it delicious – a double-decker pizza with its aromatic filling hidden between the layers.*

¾ cup (180ml) warm water

1½ teaspoons (7g) dried yeast

½ teaspoon sugar

2 cups (300g) plain flour

1 teaspoon salt

⅓ cup (80ml) olive oil

1 cup (70g) stale breadcrumbs

2 cloves garlic, crushed

1 teaspoon ground fennel

1 small red onion (100g), chopped finely

250g beef mince

100g italian salami, chopped finely

425g can crushed tomatoes

¼ cup (40g) toasted pine nuts

¼ cup coarsely chopped fresh flat-leaf parsley

½ cup (50g) finely grated fontina

1 Combine the water, yeast and sugar in small bowl, cover; stand in warm place about 10 minutes or until frothy. Combine flour and salt in large bowl, stir in yeast mixture and half of the oil; mix to a soft dough. Knead on lightly floured surface, about 5 minutes or until smooth and elastic. Place dough in large oiled bowl, cover; stand in warm place about 30 minutes or until dough doubles in size.

2 Meanwhile, heat remaining oil in large frying pan; cook breadcrumbs and half of the garlic, stirring, until crumbs are browned lightly. Remove from pan.

3 Reheat same pan; cook fennel, onion and remaining garlic, stirring, until onion softens. Add mince; cook, stirring, until mince changes colour. Stir in salami and undrained tomatoes. Bring to a boil then reduce heat; simmer, uncovered, stirring occasionally, about 15 minutes or until liquid reduces by half. Remove from heat; stir in nuts and parsley. Cool.

4 Preheat oven to hot (220°C/200°C fan-forced).

5 Punch down dough with fist; knead on lightly floured surface until smooth; divide in half. Roll each half to form 30cm round. Place one round on lightly oiled pizza or oven tray; top with breadcrumb mixture, mince mixture, cheese then remaining round. Pinch edges together; bake, uncovered, about 15 minutes or until browned lightly.

6 Stand pizza 10 minutes before cutting into wedges; serve with a rocket and parmesan salad, if desired.

**PER SERVING** 47.7g fat; 3610kJ (862 cal)

# onion focaccia

**preparation time** 20 minutes (plus standing time)  **cooking time** 25 minutes (plus cooling time)  **serves** 8

2½ cups (375g) plain flour

2 teaspoons (7g) dry yeast

¼ cup (20g) grated parmesan

2 tablespoons coarsely chopped fresh sage

3 teaspoons sea salt flakes

1 cup (250ml) warm water

¼ cup (60ml) olive oil

1 small white onion (80g), sliced thinly

1   Sift flour into large bowl; stir in yeast, cheese, sage and 1 teaspoon of the salt. Gradually stir in the water and 2 tablespoons of the oil. Knead on well-floured surface about 10 minutes or until smooth and elastic.

2   Place on greased oven tray; press into a 24cm-round. Cover with greased plastic wrap; stand in warm place until dough doubles in size.

3   Preheat oven to hot (220°C/200°C fan-forced).

4   Meanwhile, combine onion, remaining salt and remaining oil in small bowl. Remove plastic wrap from dough; sprinkle dough with onion mixture. Bake, uncovered, about 25 minutes or until cooked through; cool on wire rack.

**PER SERVING**  8.2g fat; 999kJ (239 cal)

# olive bread with oregano

**preparation time** 25 minutes (plus standing time)  **cooking time** 45 minutes (plus cooling time)  **serves** 10

1 tablespoon dry yeast

1 teaspoon sugar

2¼ cups (560ml) milk

5½ cups (825g) plain flour

⅓ cup (80ml) olive oil

1¼ cups (150g) seeded black olives, halved

2 tablespoons coarsely chopped fresh oregano

1   Combine yeast, sugar and milk in large bowl; stir in 3 cups (450g) of the flour. Cover; stand in warm place 30 minutes or until foamy. Stir in oil, then remaining flour. Knead on lightly floured surface about 10 minutes or until smooth and elastic. Place dough in large oiled bowl. Cover; stand in warm place until doubled in size.

2   Meanwhile, drain olives on absorbent paper.

3   Punch down dough with fist; knead on lightly floured surface until smooth. Knead in olives and oregano. Roll dough into 30cm x 35cm oval; fold almost in half. Place on large greased oven tray; sift 2 tablespoons of plain flour over dough.

4   Bake, uncovered, about  45 minutes or until cooked through; cool on wire rack.

**PER SERVING**  8.5g fat; 1632kJ (390 cal)

# tiramisu

**preparation time** 25 minutes (plus refrigeration time)  **serves** 6

2 tablespoons ground espresso coffee

1 cup (250ml) boiling water

½ cup (125ml) marsala

250g packet savoiardi sponge finger biscuits

300ml thickened cream

¼ cup (40g) icing sugar mixture

2 cups (500g) mascarpone cheese

2 tablespoons marsala, extra

50g dark eating chocolate, grated coarsely

1   Combine coffee and the boiling water in coffee plunger; stand 2 minutes before plunging. Combine coffee mixture and marsala in medium heatproof bowl; cool 10 minutes.

2   Place a third of the biscuits, in single layer, over base of deep 2-litre (8-cup) dish; drizzle with a third of the coffee mixture.

3   Beat cream and icing sugar mixture in small bowl until soft peaks form; transfer to large bowl. Fold in combined cheese and extra marsala.

4   Spread a third of the cream mixture over biscuits in dish. Submerge half of the remaining biscuits, one at a time, in coffee mixture, taking care the biscuits do not become so soggy that they fall apart; place over cream layer. Top biscuit layer with half of the remaining cream mixture. Repeat process with remaining biscuits, coffee mixture and cream mixture; sprinkle with chocolate. Cover; refrigerate 3 hours or overnight.

**PER SERVING**  36.3g fat; 2391kJ (572 cal)

DESSERTS

# lemon sorbetto

**preparation time** 15 minutes (plus standing and freezing time) **cooking time** 10 minutes **serves** 4

2½ cups (625ml) water

¼ cup finely grated lemon rind

1 cup (220g) caster sugar

¾ cup (180ml) lemon juice

1 egg white

1 Stir the water, rind and sugar in small saucepan over heat, without boiling, until sugar dissolves; bring to a boil. Boil, uncovered, without stirring, about 5 minutes or until syrup thickens slightly. Strain into medium heatproof jug; cool to room temperature. Stir in juice.

2 Pour sorbetto mixture into 14cm x 21cm loaf pan, cover with foil; freeze about 3 hours or until almost set.

3 Blend or process mixture with egg white until smooth. Return to pan, cover; freeze 3 hours or overnight.

TIP You can also freeze the sorbetto–egg white mixture in an ice-cream machine according to the manufacturer's instructions.

**PER SERVING** 0.1g fat; 957kJ (229 cal)

# ricotta cheesecake

**preparation time** 30 minutes (plus refrigeration and cooling time) **cooking time** 1 hour 15 minutes **serves** about 16

90g butter, softened

¼ cup (55g) caster sugar

1 egg, beaten lightly

1¼ cups (185g) plain flour

¼ cup (35g) self-raising flour

1kg ricotta

1 cup (220g) caster sugar, extra

5 eggs, beaten lightly, extra

1 tablespoon finely grated lemon rind

¼ cup (60ml) lemon juice

1 teaspoon vanilla extract

¼ cup (40g) sultanas

¼ cup (80g) finely chopped glace fruit salad

icing sugar mixture, for decorating

1 Preheat oven to moderately hot (200°C/180°C fan-forced). Grease a 28cm springform tin.

2 Beat butter in a bowl with an electric mixer until smooth but not changed in colour. Add sugar and egg; beat until just combined.

3 Stir in half the sifted flours with a wooden spoon; work remaining flour in with hands. Knead pastry gently on a lightly floured surface until smooth. Wrap in plastic; refrigerate 30 minutes.

4 Roll pastry between sheets of floured baking paper until large enough to line the base of the tin. Place the pastry in tin, press into base. Lightly prick with a fork, refrigerate 30 minutes. Cover pastry with baking paper, fill with beans or rice; bake a further 10 minutes. Remove paper and beans, bake a further 15 minutes or until browned lightly; cool.

5 Reduce oven temperature to moderately slow (160°C/140°C fan-forced).

6 Blend or process ricotta, extra sugar, extra eggs, rind, juice and vanilla until smooth. Transfer mixture to a large bowl; gently fold in sultanas and glace fruit salad. Pour ricotta mixture over pastry base.

7 Bake about 50 minutes or until filling is set; cool. Refrigerate 2 hours or until completely cooled.

8 Serve dusted with sifted icing sugar.

TIP Glace fruit salad is available from specialty food stores and some cheese counters. If unavailable, substitute glace peaches, apricots or oranges.

**PER SERVING** 13.8g fat; 1242kJ (297 cal)

# pistachio and polenta cake with blood orange syrup

**preparation time** 10 minutes  **cooking time** 1 hour 15 minutes  **serves** 12

*The blood orange, with its red-streaked, salmony-coloured flesh, is though to have occurred in nature by accident in 17th-century Sicily. In season for all too short a time in winter, blood oranges have a sweet, non-acidic pulp and juice with a slight berry taste; even the skin is not as bitter as that of other citrus.*

300g sour cream

125g butter, softened

1 cup (220g) caster sugar

2 cups (300g) self-raising flour

½ teaspoon bicarbonate of soda

⅔ cup (110g) polenta

1 teaspoon finely grated blood orange rind

¾ cup (180ml) water

⅔ cup (100g) toasted shelled pistachios

BLOOD ORANGE SYRUP

1 cup (250ml) blood orange juice

1 cup (220g) caster sugar

1 cinnamon stick

1   Preheat oven to moderately slow (160°C/140°C fan-forced). Grease deep 20cm-round cake pan; line base and side with baking paper.

2   Make blood orange syrup.

3   Place sour cream, butter, sugar, sifted flour and soda, polenta, rind and the water in large bowl; beat on low speed with electric mixer until just combined. Beat on medium speed until mixture changes to slightly lighter colour. Stir in nuts.

4   Spread cake mixture into prepared pan; bake, uncovered, about 1 hour. Stand cake in pan 10 minutes; turn cake, top-side up, onto wire rack to cool. Serve cake warm or cold with strained blood orange syrup.

BLOOD ORANGE SYRUP  Combine ingredients in small saucepan; bring to a boil, stirring. Reduce heat; simmer, uncovered, about 15 minutes or until syrup thickens. Cool to room temperature.

PER SERVING  15.2g fat; 1714kJ (412 cal)

# ricotta and mascarpone tarts with roasted pears

**preparation time** 45 mins (plus 30 minutes refrigeration time)  **cooking time** 1 hour 10 minutes  **serves** 8

1½ cups (225g) plain flour

½ cup (80g) icing sugar mixture

125g butter, chopped

1 egg

1¼ cups (250g) ricotta

½ cup (110g) caster sugar

½ cup (125g) mascarpone

2 eggs

2 teaspoons finely grated lemon rind

ROASTED PEARS

8 very small pears (1kg), peeled, quartered, cored

1 tablespoon lemon juice

⅓ cup (75g) caster sugar

1 Preheat oven to moderate (180°C/160°C fan-forced). Grease eight deep, fluted, loose-based flan tins (8cm base, 10cm top).

2 Process plain flour, icing sugar and butter until crumbly. Add egg; process until ingredients just come together. Transfer mixture to a lightly floured surface; knead gently until smooth. Wrap in plastic, refrigerate 30 minutes.

3 Divide pastry into eight portions. Roll each portion on a well-floured board into rounds large enough to line prepared tins; ease one round into each tin. Press pastry into sides; trim edges.

4 Place flan tins on two oven trays. Cover pastry with baking paper; fill with dried beans or rice. Bake 15 minutes; remove paper and beans. Bake a further 15 minutes or until pastry is golden brown. Cool 10 minutes. Reduce oven temperature to slow (150°C/130°C fan-forced).

5 Beat ricotta and sugar in small bowl with electric mixer 2 minutes or until smooth. On low speed, add mascarpone, eggs and rind; beat until combined. Pour filling into pastry cases; bake about 25 minutes or until just set. Cool to room temperature.

6 Make roasted pears. Serve tarts topped with pears.

ROASTED PEARS  Increase oven temperature to very hot (240°C/220°C fan-forced). Line baking tray with baking paper. Place the pears on prepared tray, sprinkle over lemon juice and sugar. Bake for about 15 minutes, turning occasionally, until lightly browned and tender.

TIP  We used corella pears for this recipe.

PER SERVING  26.2g fat; 2253kJ (539 cal)

# chocolate hazelnut gelato

**preparation time** 20 minutes (plus cooling and freezing time)  **cooking time** 20 minutes  **serves** 8

1 cup (125g) hazelnuts

1⅔ cups (400ml) milk

2½ cups (600ml) cream

6 egg yolks

⅓ cup (75g) caster sugar

¾ cup (215g) chocolate hazelnut spread

1   Preheat oven to moderate (180°C/160°C fan-forced). Place hazelnuts in a shallow baking dish, bake about 8 minutes or until skins begin to split and nuts are toasted. Place nuts in clean tea towel and rub vigorously to remove skins. Chop nuts coarsely. Bring milk, cream and hazelnuts to a boil in medium saucepan; cover, remove from heat. Stand 10 minutes; strain, discard hazelnuts.

2   Whisk egg yolks and sugar in medium bowl until creamy. Gradually whisk hot milk mixture into egg mixture. Return to saucepan, stir over low heat, without boiling, until mixture thickens slightly and coats back of spoon. Add chocolate hazelnut spread; whisk until combined.

3   Transfer to large bowl, press plastic wrap over surface of custard; cool slightly, refrigerate 2 hours or until cold.

4   Transfer mixture to shallow container, cover with foil and freeze until almost firm. Chop ice-cream coarsely; blend or process ice-cream until smooth. Pour into deep dish or container; cover, freeze until firm. Serve scooped in cones, if desired.

TIP   You can also freeze gelato in an ice-cream machine according to the manufacturer's instructions.

**PER SERVING**  57.2g fat; 2771kJ (663 cal)

# zabaglione

**preparation time** 5 minutes  **cooking time** 15 minutes  **serves** 6

2 eggs

4 egg yolks

½ cup (110g) caster sugar

⅓ cup (80ml) marsala

12 savoiardi sponge finger biscuits

1   Place eggs, yolks and sugar in large heatproof bowl over pan of simmering water, ensuring the water does not touch bottom of bowl.

2   With an electric hand mixer or whisk, beat egg mixture constantly until light and fluffy. Gradually add marsala while continuing to whisk about 10 minutes or until mixture is thick and creamy.

3   Spoon zabaglione into small serving glasses; serve with sponge fingers.

**PER SERVING**  6.6g fat; 961kJ (230 cal)

# panna cotta with roasted nectarines

preparation time 25 minutes (plus refrigeration time) **cooking time** 20 minutes **serves** 4

300ml thickened cream

1 cup (250ml) milk

1 vanilla bean, split

¼ cup (55g) caster sugar

1½ teaspoons gelatine

1 strip lemon rind

ROASTED NECTARINES

4 medium nectarines (680g), halved, seeded

⅓ cup (75g) caster sugar

½ cup (125ml) dessert wine

1   Combine cream, milk, vanilla bean, sugar, gelatine and rind in pan; stir over low heat until warm. Stand until cool.

2   Strain cream mixture through fine strainer into medium jug; discard vanilla pod. Pour mixture into 4 x ½-cup capacity moulds. Cover; refrigerate 6 hours or overnight.

3   Make roasted nectarines.

4   Turn out panna cotta; serve with nectarines and pan juices.

ROASTED NECTARINES  Preheat oven to hot (220°C/200°C fan-forced). Place nectarines, cut-side up, in small ovenproof dish; sprinkle with sugar and drizzle with wine. Roast 15 minutes or until browned lightly and softened. Cool.

PER SERVING  30.5g fat; 2282kJ (546 cal)

**ARBORIO RICE** small, round-grain rice well suited to absorb a large amount of liquid; the high level of starch makes it especially suitable for risotto, giving the dish its classic creaminess.

**ARTICHOKES**
**globe** large flower bud of a member of the thistle family; it has tough petal-like leaves and is edible in part when cooked.
**hearts** tender centre of the globe artichoke. Artichoke hearts can be harvested fresh from the plant after the prickly choke is removed. Available in brine in cans or glass jars.

**BAY LEAVES** aromatic leaves from the bay tree available fresh or dried; used to add a strong, slightly peppery flavour to soups, stocks, casseroles and meat or fish dishes.

**BEANS**
**borlotti** also known as roman beans or pink beans. Interchangeable with pinto beans because of the similarity in appearance. Both are pale pink or beige with dark red streaks. The bean of choice for refried beans in Mexican cookery.
**cannellini** small white bean similar in looks and flavour to other *phaseolus vulgaris* varieties (great northern, navy or haricot). Available dried and canned. Used in baked beans and in traditional ham and bean soup.

**BEEF**
**chuck steak** inexpensive cut from the neck and shoulder area; good minced and slow-cooked.

**BLACK PEPPER** the true pepper, *Piper nigrum*. It is economically the most important species of pan-tropical pepper. Native to Java, it was introduced into other tropical countries. A climbing shrub, it bears fruits (peppercorns) the size of peas. Black pepper, which is sold whole, ground or cracked, is the dried whole fruit. White pepper, made by removing the dark outer hull, has a less biting flavour.

**BREADS**
**ciabatta** in Italian, the word means slipper, which is the traditional shape of this popular crisp-crusted white bread.
**sourdough** so-named, not because it has a sour taste, but because it's made by using a small amount of 'starter dough', which contains a yeast culture, mixed into flour and water. Part of the dough is saved to use as the starter dough next time.

**CAPERS** the grey-green buds of a warm climate (usually Mediterranean) shrub. They are sold either dried and salted or pickled in a vinegar brine; tiny young ones, called baby capers, are also available both in brine or dried in salt. Their pungent taste adds piquancy to a classic steak tartare and to tapenade, sauces and various condiments.

**CAPSICUM** this is also known as pepper or bell pepper. It is native to central and South America. Available in purplish-black, red, green, yellow or orange. Both the seeds and the membranes must be discarded before use.

**CHEESE**
**bocconcini** from the word 'boccone', meaning mouthful in Italian; walnut-sized baby mozzarella, a delicate, semi-soft, white cheese traditionally made from buffalo milk. Sold fresh, it spoils rapidly so will only keep, refrigerated in brine, for 1 or 2 days at the most.
**fetta** crumbly goat- or sheep-milk cheese with a sharp, salty taste.
**fontina** a smooth, firm Italian cow-milk cheese with a red or brown rind. It has a creamy, nutty taste; an ideal melting or grilling cheese.
**gorgonzola** creamy Italian blue cheese with a mild, sweet taste; a good accompaniment to fruit and as a flavouring for sauces (especially pasta).
**mozzarella** soft, spun-curd cheese traditionally made from buffalo milk. Now generally made from cow milk, it is the most popular cheese for pizzas, with a low melting point and considerable elasticity when heated. Used for texture rather than flavour.
**parmesan** also known as parmigiano, parmesan is a hard, grainy cow-milk cheese which originated in the Parma region of Italy. The curd for this cheese is salted in brine for a month before being aged for up to two years, preferably in humid conditions. Parmesan is grated or flaked and used for pasta, salads and soups; it is also eaten with fruit. Reggiano is the best parmesan; it is aged for a minimum of 2 years and made only in the Italian region of Emilia-Romagna.
**provolone** a mild stretched-curd cheese which is similar to mozzarella when young. It becomes harder, spicier and grainy the longer it is aged. Golden yellow in colour, with a smooth waxy rind, provolone is a good all-purpose cheese to be used in cooking, for dessert with cheese, and shredded or flaked.
**ricotta** soft, white, cow-milk cheese. A sweet, moist cheese with a slightly grainy texture and a fat content of around 8.5 per cent. The name roughly translates as 'cooked again' and refers to the method of

GLOSSARY

manufacture. The cheese is made from a whey that is itself a by-product of other cheese making.

**romano** a hard cheese made from cow or sheep milk. Straw-coloured and grainy in texture, it is mainly used for grating. Parmesan can be used as an alternative.

## CHILLI

**cayenne pepper** a thin-fleshed, long, extremely hot, dried red chilli, it is usually purchased ground; both arbol and guajillo chillies are the fresh sources for cayenne.

**chipotle** pronounced cheh-pot-ley. The name used for jalapeño chillies once they've been dried and smoked.

**jalapeño** pronounced hah-lah-pain-yo. Fairly hot, medium-sized, plump, dark green chilli, available pickled, sold canned or bottled, and fresh, from specialty greengrocers.

**thai red** small, medium hot chilli, bright red in colour.

## EGGPLANT

also known as aubergine. Often thought of as a vegetable but it is actually a fruit belonging to the same family as the tomato, chilli and potato. Ranges from tiny to very large and from pale green to deep purple. Purchased fresh as well as char-grilled, packed in oil, in jars.

## FENNEL

also known as finocchio or anise. This crunchy green vegetable, which slightly resembles celery, can be eaten raw or braised or fried. It has an aniseed or licorice flavour. Dried fennel seeds have a more pronounced flavour.

## KUMARA

Polynesian name of orange-fleshed sweet potato; often confused with yam.

## MUSHROOMS

**button** small, cultivated, mild-flavoured white mushroom.

**dried porcini** also known as cepes; the mushroom with the richest flavour. Expensive, but because they are so strongly flavoured, only a small amount is required in any dish. Use in risottos and stews.

**oyster** also known as abalone; grey-white mushroom shaped like a fan. They are prized for their smooth texture and their very subtle, oyster-like flavour.

**shiitake** fresh shiitake are also known as chinese black, forest or golden oak mushrooms. They are large and meaty, with the earthiness and taste of wild mushrooms. Dried shiitake are also known as donko or dried chinese mushrooms; rehydrate in warm water before use.

**swiss brown** a light to dark brown mushroom with a full-bodied flavour.

## ONIONS

**green** also known as scallion or, incorrectly, shallot; an immature onion picked before the bulb has formed, having a long, bright-green edible stalk.

**red** also known as spanish, red spanish or bermuda onion; a sweet-flavoured, large, purple-red onion.

## PARSLEY, FLAT-LEAF

also known as continental or italian parsley.

## PASTA

**angel hair** also called barbina. This pasta is in very fine strands.

**farfalle** bow-tie shaped short pasta; sometimes known as butterfly pasta.

**fresh lasagne sheets** thinly rolled wide sheets of plain or flavoured pasta; they do not require par-boiling prior to being used in cooking.

**gnocchi** Italian 'dumplings' made of potatoes, semolina or flour; can be cooked in boiling water or baked with a sauce.

**orecchiette** translates as 'little ears'. A small, disc-shaped pasta.

**pappardelle** wide, ribbonlike pasta with scalloped edges.

**risoni** also known as risi; small, rice-shaped pasta that is similar to orzo, another small pasta.

**tagliatelle** long, flat strips of durum wheat pasta, narrower and thinner than fettuccine.

**tortellini** circles of fresh plain pasta that are stuffed with a meat or cheese filling and then folded into a shape resembling a little hat.

## PASTA SAUCE

a ready-made tomato-based sauce (may be called ragu or sugo on the label). It is available in varying degrees of thickness and with different flavourings such as basil or garlic.

## PINE NUTS

also known as pignoli; not a nut, in fact, but a small, cream-coloured kernel from pine cones. Best roasted before use to bring out the delicate nutty flavour.

## POLENTA

a flour-like cereal made of dried corn (maize). It is also known as cornmeal. The name polenta is also given to the dish made from this cereal.

## PROSCIUTTO

a type of un-smoked Italian ham which is salted, air-cured and aged; it is usually eaten uncooked. Of the many styles of prosciutto, one of the best is Parma ham, from Italy's Emilia-Romagna region; it is traditionally lightly salted and dried and then eaten raw.

## ROCKET

also known as rugula, arugula and rucola; a peppery green leaf eaten raw in salads or used in cooking. Baby rocket leaves are smaller and have a less peppery taste.

## SAVOY CABBAGE

a fairly mild-tasting cabbage; has a large, heavy head with crinkled dark-green outer leaves.

## SPATCHCOCK

a small chicken (poussin), which is no more than 6 weeks old and weighs a maximum of 500g. Spatchcock is also a term used to describe splitting open a small chicken, then flattening and grilling it.

## SPECK

smoked pork.

## SPONGE FINGER BISCUITS

also known as savoiardi, savoy biscuits or lady's finger biscuits; these Italian-style crisp fingers are made from a sponge-cake mixture.

## SQUID

a type of mollusc, also known as calamari. Buy squid hoods to make preparation and cooking faster.

## SWORDFISH

also known as broadbill. Yellowfin or bluefin tuna or mahi mahi can be used in place of swordfish.

## TUNA

reddish, firm-fleshed fish; slightly dry. Many varieties are available including bluefin, yellowfin, skipjack or albacore.

## VINEGAR

**balsamic** originally a term given to a wine-based vinegar made in Modena, Italy. Many balsamic vinegars from other areas are now on the market. They range in pungency and quality depending on how, and for how long, they have been aged. Up to a point, quality can be determined by price; use the most expensive ones sparingly.

**cider** made from fermented apples.

**sherry** mellow wine vinegar named for its colour.

## YEAST

(dried and fresh), a raising agent used in dough making. This organism grows best in warm, moist conditions; over-hot dissolving liquid or a hot room temperature will kill yeast and stop the dough from rising. Either granular (7g sachets) or fresh compressed pieces (20g) can be used when yeast is required in a recipe.

## A

anchovies
anchovy and garlic tuna with tomato and oregano 79
onion, anchovy and olive pizzetta 95
artichokes
mushroom, pea and artichoke risotto 41
veal with artichokes, olives and lemon 60
asparagus and prawn risotto 38

## B

baby zucchini with garlic crumbs 91
baked ricotta, herbed 15
basil
chicken stuffed with ricotta, basil and prosciutto 67
dressing 91
tapenade 29
beans
celery and bean salad 83
tuscan bean soup 19
tuscan white bean salad 84
beef stew, tuscan 52
braised pork with pancetta and fennel 63
bruschetta with eggplant and olive topping 7

## C

cake, pistachio and polenta, with blood orange syrup 108
calves liver, venetian, and onions 56
cannelloni, chicken and prosciutto 33
caprese salad 88
capsicums, marinated 12
carbonara, fettuccine 25
carpaccio with fennel salad 8
celery and bean salad 83
char-grilled squid with rocket and parmesan salad 72
char-grilled vegetable stack with basil sauce 91
cheese
cheesy pesto polenta 41
vegetable gnocchi with cheese sauce 37
cheesecake, ricotta 107
chicken
chicken and prosciutto cannelloni 33
chicken cacciatore with split pea salad 64
chicken stuffed with ricotta, basil and prosciutto 67
white wine risotto cakes with smoked chicken 42
chilli and garlic spaghettini with breadcrumbs 30

chocolate hazelnut gelato 112
clams, spaghetti with 30

## E

eggplant
bruschetta with olive topping and 7
marinated 12

## F

fennel salad, carpaccio with 8
fetta
fig and fetta mini toasts 4
marinated 4
fettuccine carbonara 25
figs
fig and fetta mini toasts 4
fig, prosciutto and goat cheese pizzetta 96
fish fillets, pan-fried, with pancetta and caper herb butter 76
focaccia, onion 103
frittata with two toppings 11

## G

gelato, chocolate hazelnut 112
gnocchi
three sauces, with 34
vegetable, with cheese sauce 37
gremolata 48
seafood soup with 21
grilled herb polenta with semi-dried tomato and olive salad 46
grilled vegetables and basil tapenade pasta 29

## K

kingfish with salsa verde and white bean puree 68

## L

lamb with white wine and mascarpone sauce 59
lasagne bolognese 26
lemon sorbetto 107

## M

marinated capsicums 12
marinated eggplants 12
marinated mushrooms 12
mascarpone
lamb with white wine and mascarpone sauce 59
ricotta and mascarpone tarts with roasted pears 111
mayonnaise, spiced 46
minestrone alla milanese 16
mini toasts, fig and fetta 4
mussels with garlic crumbs 15

## N

napoletana pizza 92
nectarines, roasted 115

## O

octopus braised in red wine 71
orecchiette boscaiola 29
osso buco with semi-dried tomatoes and olives 48

## P

pancetta
braised pork with pancetta and fennel 63
fish fillets with pancetta and caper herb butter 76
panna cotta with roasted nectarines 115
panzanella 87
pea, mushroom and artichoke risotto 41
pears, roasted 111
penne puttanesca with mushrooms 25
pesto
cheesy pesto polenta 41
classic 34
slow-roasted pesto salmon 75
pistachio and polenta cake with blood orange syrup 108
pizza 92–103
basic pizza dough 92
napoletana 92
potato and rosemary 99
sicilian stuffed pizza 100
pizzetta
fig, prosciutto and goat cheese 96
onion, anchovy and olive 95
polenta
cheesy pesto 41
creamy, with slow-roasted mushrooms 45
grilled herb, with semi-dried tomato and olive salad 46
pistachio and polenta cake with blood orange syrup 108
pork, braised, with pancetta and fennel 63
potato and rosemary pizza 99
prawn and asparagus risotto 38
prosciutto
chicken and prosciutto cannelloni 33
chicken stuffed with ricotta, basil and prosciutto 67
fig, prosciutto and goat cheese pizzetta 96
prosciutto-wrapped spatchcocks with lemon and sage 59

## R

ricotta
cheesecake 107
chicken stuffed with ricotta, basil and prosciutto 67
herbed baked 15
ricotta and mascarpone tarts with roasted pears 111
risotto
mushroom, pea and artichoke 41
prawn and asparagus 38
saltimbocca with risotto milanese 55
white wine risotto cakes with smoked chicken 42

## S

salads 84–91
caprese 88
celery and bean 83
olive 46
tuscan white bean salad 84
salmon, slow-roasted pesto 75
salsa verde 68
saltimbocca with risotto milanese 55
sauce
basic tomato pizza sauce 92
basil 91
three-cheese 35
tomato 35
seafood soup with gremolata 21
sicilian stuffed pizza 100
sorbetto, lemon 107
spaghetti napoletana 22
spaghetti with clams 30
spaghettini, chilli and garlic, with breadcrumbs 30
spatchcocks, prosciutto-wrapped, with lemon and sage 59
split pea salad, chicken cacciatore with 64
squid, char-grilled, with rocket and parmesan salad 72
stracciatella 19
swordfish with celery and bean salad 83

## T

tarts, ricotta and mascarpone, with roasted pears 111
tiella 88
tiramisu 104
tomatoes
anchovy and garlic tuna with tomato and oregano 79
basic tomato pizza sauce 92
osso buco with semi-dried tomatoes and olives 48
semi-dried tomato and olive salad 46
tomato sauce 35
tuna, anchovy and garlic, with tomato and oregano 79
tuscan bean soup 19
tuscan beef stew 52
tuscan white bean salad 84

## V

veal
artichokes, olives and lemon, with 60
veal scaloppine with potato fennel gratin 51
vegetable gnocchi with cheese sauce 37
vegetables 84–91
char-grilled vegetable stack with basil sauce 91
grilled vegetables and basil tapenade pasta 29
venetian calves liver and onions 56

## W

white bean salad, tuscan 84
white wine risotto cakes with smoked chicken 42

## Z

zabaglione 112
zucchini, baby, with garlic 91

INDEX

## MEASURES

One Australian metric measuring cup holds approximately 250ml; one Australian metric tablespoon holds 20ml; one Australian metric teaspoon holds 5ml.

The difference between one country's measuring cups and another's is within a two- or three-teaspoon variance, and will not affect your cooking results. North America, New Zealand and the United Kingdom use a 15ml tablespoon.

All cup and spoon measurements are level. The most accurate way of measuring dry ingredients is to weigh them. When measuring liquids, use a clear glass or plastic jug with the metric markings.

We use large eggs with an average weight of 60g.

## DRY MEASURES

| METRIC | IMPERIAL |
|---|---|
| 15g | ½oz |
| 30g | 1oz |
| 60g | 2oz |
| 90g | 3oz |
| 125g | 4oz (¼lb) |
| 155g | 5oz |
| 185g | 6oz |
| 220g | 7oz |
| 250g | 8oz (½lb) |
| 280g | 9oz |
| 315g | 10oz |
| 345g | 11oz |
| 375g | 12oz (¾lb) |
| 410g | 13oz |
| 440g | 14oz |
| 470g | 15oz |
| 500g | 16oz (1lb) |
| 750g | 24oz (1½lb) |
| 1kg | 32oz (2lb) |

## LIQUID MEASURES

| METRIC | IMPERIAL |
|---|---|
| 30ml | 1 fluid oz |
| 60ml | 2 fluid oz |
| 100ml | 3 fluid oz |
| 125ml | 4 fluid oz |
| 150ml | 5 fluid oz (¼ pint/1 gill) |
| 190ml | 6 fluid oz |
| 250ml | 8 fluid oz |
| 300ml | 10 fluid oz (½ pint) |
| 500ml | 16 fluid oz |
| 600ml | 20 fluid oz (1 pint) |
| 1000ml (1 litre) | 1¾ pints |

## LENGTH MEASURES

| METRIC | IMPERIAL |
|---|---|
| 3mm | ⅛in |
| 6mm | ¼in |
| 1cm | ½in |
| 2cm | ¾in |
| 2.5cm | 1in |
| 5cm | 2in |
| 6cm | 2½in |
| 8cm | 3in |
| 10cm | 4in |
| 13cm | 5in |
| 15cm | 6in |
| 18cm | 7in |
| 20cm | 8in |
| 23cm | 9in |
| 25cm | 10in |
| 28cm | 11in |
| 30cm | 12in (1ft) |

## OVEN TEMPERATURES

These oven temperatures are only a guide for conventional ovens.
For fan-forced ovens, check the manufacturer's manual.

| | °C (CELSIUS) | °F (FAHRENHEIT) | GAS MARK |
|---|---|---|---|
| Very slow | 120 | 250 | ½ |
| Slow | 150 | 275-300 | 1-2 |
| Moderately slow | 170 | 325 | 3 |
| Moderate | 180 | 350-375 | 4-5 |
| Moderately hot | 200 | 400 | 6 |
| Hot | 220 | 425-450 | 7-8 |
| Very hot | 240 | 475 | 9 |

# CONVERSION CHART

# ARE YOU MISSING SOME OF THE WORLD'S FAVOURITE COOKBOOKS?

*The Australian Women's Weekly* Cookbooks are available from bookshops, cookshops, supermarkets and other stores all over the world. You can also buy direct from the publisher, using the order form below.

| TITLE | RRP | QTY | TITLE | RRP | QTY |
|---|---|---|---|---|---|
| Asian, Meals in Minutes | £6.99 | | Japanese Cooking Class | £6.99 | |
| Babies & Toddlers Good Food | £6.99 | | Kids' Birthday Cakes | £6.99 | |
| Barbecue Meals In Minutes | £6.99 | | Kids Cooking | £6.99 | |
| Beginners Cooking Class | £6.99 | | Lean Food | £6.99 | |
| Beginners Simple Meals | £6.99 | | Low-carb, Low-fat | £6.99 | |
| Beginners Thai | £6.99 | | Low-fat Feasts | £6.99 | |
| Best Food | £6.99 | | Low-fat Food For Life | £6.99 | |
| Best Food Desserts | £6.99 | | Low-fat Meals in Minutes | £6.99 | |
| Best Food Fast | £6.99 | | Main Course Salads | £6.99 | |
| Best Food Mains | £6.99 | | Mexican | £6.99 | |
| Cakes Biscuits & Slices | £6.99 | | Middle Eastern Cooking Class | £6.99 | |
| Cakes Cooking Class | £6.99 | | Midweek Meals in Minutes | £6.99 | |
| Caribbean Cooking | £6.99 | | Muffins, Scones & Breads | £6.99 | |
| Casseroles | £6.99 | | New Casseroles | £6.99 | |
| Chicken | £6.99 | | New Classics | £6.99 | |
| Chicken Meals in Minutes | £6.99 | | New Finger Food | £6.99 | |
| Chinese Cooking Class | £6.99 | | New Salads (Oct 06) | £6.99 | |
| Christmas Cooking | £6.99 | | Party Food and Drink | £6.99 | |
| Chocolate | £6.99 | | Pasta Meals in Minutes | £6.99 | |
| Cocktails | £6.99 | | Potatoes | £6.99 | |
| Cooking for Friends | £6.99 | | Salads: Simple, Fast & Fresh | £6.99 | |
| Detox | £6.99 | | Saucery | £6.99 | |
| Dinner Beef | £6.99 | | Sauces Salsas & Dressings | £6.99 | |
| Dinner Lamb | £6.99 | | Sensational Stir-Fries | £6.99 | |
| Dinner Seafood | £6.99 | | Short-order Cook | £6.99 | |
| Easy Australian Style | £6.99 | | Slim | £6.99 | |
| Easy Curry | £6.99 | | Stir-fry | £6.99 | |
| Easy Spanish-Style | £6.99 | | Superfoods for Exam Success | £6.99 | |
| Essential Soup | £6.99 | | Sweet Old Fashioned Favourites | £6.99 | |
| French Food, New | £6.99 | | Tapas Mezze Antipasto & other bites | £6.99 | |
| Fresh Food for Babies & Toddlers | £6.99 | | Thai Cooking Class | £6.99 | |
| Get Real, Make a Meal | £6.99 | | Traditional Italian | £6.99 | |
| Good Food Fast | £6.99 | | Vegetarian Meals in Minutes | £6.99 | |
| Great Lamb Cookbook | £6.99 | | Vegie Food | £6.99 | |
| Greek Cooking Class | £6.99 | | Weekend Cook | £6.99 | |
| Grills | £6.99 | | Wicked Sweet Indulgences | £6.99 | |
| Healthy Heart Cookbook | £6.99 | | Wok, Meals in Minutes | £6.99 | |
| Indian Cooking Class | £6.99 | | TOTAL COST: | £ | |

Mr/Mrs/Ms _____

Address _____

_____ Postcode _____

Day time phone _____ Email* (optional) _____

I enclose my cheque/money order for £ _____

or please charge £ _____

to my:  ☐ Access  ☐ Mastercard  ☐ Visa  ☐ Diners Club

PLEASE NOTE: WE DO NOT ACCEPT SWITCH OR ELECTRON CARDS

Card number ☐☐☐☐ ☐☐☐☐ ☐☐☐☐ ☐☐☐☐

Expiry date _____ 3 digit security code *(found on reverse of card)* _____

Cardholder's name_____ Signature _____

**To order:** Mail or fax – photocopy or complete the order form above, and send your credit card details or cheque payable to: Australian Consolidated Press (UK), Moulton Park Business Centre, Red House Road, Moulton Park, Northampton NN3 6AQ, phone (+44) (0) 1604 497531 fax (+44) (0) 1604 497533, e-mail books@acpmedia.co.uk or order online at www.acpuk.com

**Non-UK residents:** We accept the credit cards listed on the coupon, or cheques, drafts or International Money Orders payable in sterling and drawn on a UK bank. Credit card charges are at the exchange rate current at the time of payment.

**Postage and packing UK:** Add £1.00 per order plus 50p per book.

**Postage and packing overseas:** Add £2.00 per order plus £1.00 per book.

All pricing current at time of going to press and subject to change/availability.

**Offer ends 31.12.2007**

* By including your email address, you consent to receipt of any email regarding this magazine, and other emails which inform you of ACP's other publications, products, services and events, and to promote third party goods and services you may be interested in.